How Many?

How Many?

A COUNTING BOOK / TEACHER'S GUIDE

CHRISTOPHER DANIELSON

STENHOUSE PUBLISHERS
PORTLAND, MAINE

Stenhouse Publishers
www.stenhouse.com

Library of Congress Cataloging-in-Publication Data

Names: Danielson, Christopher, author.
Title: How many? : a counting book : teacher's guide / Christopher Danielson.
Description: [Teacher's edition]. | Portland, Maine : Stenhouse Publishers,
   [2018] | Includes bibliographical references.
Identifiers: LCCN 2018004791 (print) | LCCN 2018008818 (ebook) | ISBN
   9781625312198 (ebook) | ISBN 9781625312181 (pbk. (sold as bundle with
   hardcover student book) : alk. paper)
Subjects: LCSH: Counting--Problems, exercises, etc. | Counting--Study and
   teaching. | Mathematics--Study and teaching.
Classification: LCC QA113 (ebook) | LCC QA113 .D37225b 2018 (print) | DDC
   513.2/11--dc23
LC record available at https://lccn.loc.gov/2018004791

Book design by Blue Design (www.bluedes.com)
Manufactured in the United States of America

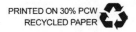
PRINTED ON 30% PCW
RECYCLED PAPER

24 23 22 21 20 19 18   9 8 7 6 5 4 3 2 1

For my mother, who nurtured my creativity,
and for my father, who nurtured my logic. I hope you
both see the best of yourselves in my work.

CONTENTS

Acknowledgments

I am grateful to the whole Stenhouse team—especially to Tracy Zager for good humor, patience, a critical eye, and for just generally getting me and my work, and to Dan Tobin and Toby Gordon for seeing the potential in a series of books of mathematical ambiguity.

Thank you Scott Dorrance and Lorie Dorrance for the beautiful images, and to Tom Morgan for putting everything together so it looks amazing. Thank you also to the Stenhouse production team—Jay Kilburn, Louisa Irele, Vicki Rosenzweig, and Andre Barnett—for attending to precision, persevering in solving the problems I present, and all the other practices (mathematical or not) that have made the final product better than I could have imagined.

This book would not exist without the influence of a number of people who taught me to see in new ways, most of all Dan Meyer, Karim Ani, Vi Hart, Jenny Wales, Malke Rosenfeld, and Tana Hoban.

Thanks also go to Laura Wagenman and the teachers and students of the Osseo Area Schools who hosted me at various phases of writing this book. Thanks to Debbie Nichols and your wonderful students for inviting me into your classroom and your thinking. My ideas and questions are better because of you.

And thank you Rachel, Griffin, and Tabitha for your patience, love, and support.

Sign-In Information

To access the book's digital content on sten.pub/HowMany, please enter the code UNITCHAT.

CHAPTER 1

Why Another Counting Book?

My children, Griffin and Tabitha (eight and five years old at the time), were discussing the day's activities a while back. For Tabitha, the highlight of the day had been making brownies with her mother. Griffin asked, "How many brownies did you make?"

"One big one!" Tabitha replied. "Mommy cut it up."

As a math teacher and a father, I have a deep fondness for the mathematical minds of children. Furthermore, I delight in the opportunities that children's everyday worlds present for stimulating their math minds. In the case of this story, Griffin and Tabitha had different ideas about what makes a brownie. Is a brownie like a cake in that the whole pan is a single thing and then you cut it up into pieces? This was Tabitha's view. Or is a brownie like a slice of cake, a unit that you create by cutting up the larger thing? This was Griffin's view. For me, determining who is right is much less interesting than noticing the difference in perspective. This difference is summed up by the question, "What counts as one?" My job in this Teacher's Guide is to convince you that "What counts as one?" is one of the most important questions in elementary school mathematics.

Not only is "What counts as one?" an important question, its answer changes based on your perspective, and so it offers opportunities for play. Children like to play; they need to play. Their need to play with ideas is no different from their need for physical play. Children find numbers wonderful, delightful, interesting, and fun. Numbers constitute a playground for children's minds. *How Many?* is a book I designed to elicit wonder and delight in children, which they will then share with their families and teachers.

Much of this delight and wonder comes from the relationship between math and children's everyday worlds. The relationship goes both ways. Children's worlds are sources of mathematical inquiry, and developing mathematical knowledge gives them new perspectives on their worlds. I designed the images in *How Many?* in this spirit. The photographs of ordinary objects arranged with mathematical structure in mind allow children to see these objects in new ways and then to look at their world with new perspective, just as the story of the ambiguous brownies did for me. I now see brownies differently because of my children's conversation, and this conversation was one of many that made me question whether one is always one.

Traditional counting books have a less ambitious agenda. Traditionally, counting books tell you what to count—*what counts as one* is predetermined. They tell you how many there are on each page, and the pages are in numerical order. One dog is followed by two cats, then three birds and so on, usually ending at ten, sometimes at twelve. The only suspense arises from what you'll count on the next page, the only tension from the challenge of a slightly greater number. The best of these books (e.g., *Quack and Count*, or *Mouse Count*) incorporates a wonderful narrative, but, even in these rare cases, the story tends to be more important than the math in moving the book along.

How Many? is different. It is a counting book with layers, one that proceeds by presenting increasingly sophisticated mathematical opportunities. *How Many?* is a book that tells you very little, yet draws you in and invites you to linger, to ask questions, and to converse.

Each two-page spread in *How Many?* consists of the one simple question from the title and a photograph. The first photo is of a pair of shoes in a box (Figure 1.1). Your answer to the question "How many?" depends on what you are counting. Do you see two shoes or one pair of shoes? Maybe your answer to "How many?" is "one" but for a different reason; maybe you see one box or one dodecagon. (A *dodecagon* is a twelve-sided polygon. Now that you know there are some in Figure 1.1, can you find any?) If you spend a moment and look more closely, you'll notice more things to count and get more answers to the question, "How many?" You may count eyelets (twenty) or aglets (the hard plastic bits on the ends of the shoelaces; there are four of these) or yellow stitches

FIGURE 1.1
Your answer to "How many?" depends on what you decide to count.

or pinholes on the insoles of the shoes.

On the next page, the box is empty. For many of the things you counted on the first page, the answer to "How many?" is now zero. But removing the shoes reveals footprints, of which there are two, and which are subdivided into many small parts of various sizes and shapes.

Proceeding through the book, you will encounter eggs, avocados, grapefruit, and pizza. The numbers don't just get bigger; they get more interesting and nuanced. The ambiguity of the prompt allows you to think and wonder. Does cheese count as a pizza topping? Does sauce? What is the plural of pepperoni? How much juice can you get from half a grapefruit? Are a dozen half-eggs the same as half-a-dozen eggs? These questions (and more . . . so many more) naturally arise in the classrooms I've visited to ask, "How many?"

A couple of years after the ambiguous brownie conversation, friend and online colleague Ashli Black tweeted me a photograph of twenty-four half-avocados in a 6-by-4 array. I was teaching a math class for future elementary and special education teachers in which we had been studying multiplication in general and arrays in particular. I thought I would show this photo to my class as an example of turning a playful mathematical eye on the world. Instead, this book was born. My students counted pits and divots, wholes and halves, rows and columns, and batches of guacamole. We had a rich twenty-minute mathematical conversation provoked by a single image. The avocado array in *How Many?* (Figure 1.2) is a homage to this original and a tribute to my students' ingenuity. I now know that that day in my classroom was no aberration. Given a well-structured image, an open prompt, and time to think, all classrooms can have extended conversations about counting, numbers, and different ways of understanding the world numerically. *How Many?* provides the prompt and the well-structured images. I invite you and your students to take the time to think together.

A well-structured *How Many?* image has multiple ways to count the same thing. It's not just that you can count both shoes and shoeboxes—you can count the shoes themselves in at least two different ways: individually or as a pair. You can count avocados or half-avocados, eggs or dozens of eggs. Units shift in *How Many?* by drawing on the reader's everyday experience. We are used to thinking of shoes in pairs, and of eggs in dozens, so these different units (shoe, pair, egg, dozen) arise naturally in conversations about the photos in the book.

Seeing the same thing two ways matters for children's learning about numbers. Place value, for example, is built on putting things into groups. Why does 20 have a 2 in it? Because there are two groups of ten. Children who have not had rich experiences with making and breaking up groups tend to think of 20 without this structure. For them,

twenty is the word after nineteen, and you write it as a 2 and a 0. This surface understanding leads to fragile mastery of facts and algorithms in the best of cases, and all too commonly to lifelong avoidance of mathematics altogether. But these sad outcomes are unnecessary. All children can learn to use groups and units to build powerful mathematical ideas, and *How Many?* can provide a playful launching pad.

I used to think that the size of the groups that children encountered in the

FIGURE 1.2
An array of avocado halves

world mattered for their later learning about place value. I thought children might be better equipped to understand place value if eggs came in tens because I thought ten-ness was the essence of place value. I no longer think that. I now understand that *groups* are the essence of place value. What matters for their learning is that children have experiences with standard-sized groups of things. Eggs are a particularly handy example of groups, rather than an unfortunate group of twelve. What matters is that children know that eggs tend to come in groups of a particular size, that the word *dozen* refers to this group, and that you can have one dozen, or two dozens, or a dozen dozens. What matters is that children have experiences building new units out of groups of familiar units and new, larger units out of groups of these groups.

Likewise, understanding of place value to the right of the decimal point (e.g., 0.5 or 1.002) is best supported by lots of opportunity to cut things into equal-sized pieces, and this partitioning experience is far more important than whether children have experiences cutting things into ten pieces. In addition to the opportunities to work with units and groups, *How Many?* invites play with partitioning to make new units, with half-avocados, slices of pizza, and an entire page dedicated to halves.

In this Teacher's Guide, I share what I've learned from research, classrooms, and conversations with learners of all ages about how people develop an understanding of numbers, counting, and place value. I use the prompts from *How Many?* as a context for understanding children's ideas about numbers, and I look beyond these prompts to extensions and even distant mathematical horizons.

Chapter 2 is where you can learn about research on children's learning of number structure and place value. In Chapter 3, I highlight strategies for using *How Many?* in the classroom, including connecting the prompts and ideas to classroom routines and curriculum structures you may already have in place. In Chapter 4, I report on the conversations I've had in classrooms stemming from these prompts and shine a light on the beautiful mathematics that underlies children's ways of viewing and talking about them. In short, Chapter 4 is the place where I invite you into the mathematical world of children. In Chapter 5, I offer answers to the question *How Many?* for each page in the book. I do not promise that Chapter 5 is the final word on the right number of all possible things that children can count on each page. Instead, the answers in Chapter 5 are intended to give you a starting place for understanding the diversity of ideas your students are likely to express and to provide opportunities for you to push their thinking when that's necessary. Throughout the book, I'll share my experiences and learning from my long journey into understanding how children learn about numbers, and I'll raise questions for you to investigate together with your own students.

I was ready to learn with my students on the day of the avocado array because I had been working for years to understand what it means to learn about ideas such as multiplication and place value. I hope that wherever you are in your own math learning journey, *How Many?* will find you ready to learn something together with your students. There is much to learn, and this Teacher's Guide covers a lot of ground, so I feel confident you'll find useful insights here, and I hope that conversations in your classroom will provide new questions that will make you want to return for a closer read.

CHAPTER 2
Number Learning

Before outlining research on how children learn the mathematics embedded in *How Many?*, I'd like to work on some foundational questions, namely, *What is mathematics?* and *Why do we teach it in school?* These two questions are at the heart of a common refrain in math classrooms (especially in secondary schools)—*When am I ever going to use this?*

This last question asks the teacher to justify the time and attention being invested. Likely most students asking this question really want to know, *Why do I need to know this?* and they presume (or have previously heard) the answer, *Because it is useful.* While it may feel like a distraction in the moment, *When am I ever going to use this?* is precisely the sort of question we want our fellow citizens in a democracy to expect an answer to. We should honor the spirit of the question and do our best to offer an honest answer.

In fact, we math teachers would do well to answer a related question for ourselves: *Why am I teaching this?* When it comes to mathematics, my answer to that question has two parts.

First, there is a set of practical quantitative and spatial skills necessary for informed participation in society. We ought to view learning these skills as both a civil right and an obligation. I'm thinking here about number sense and estimation; fluent computation; basic understandings of variables; ways of representing relationships between variables (such as graphs, tables, and equations); ways of subdividing and rearranging one-, two-, and three-dimensional space; and basic data analysis and probability.

Second, math is one of several bodies of knowledge that we have agreed as a society are important. To be educated means knowing and having experienced certain ideas and techniques of the arts and sciences. In this way, we pass on our culture. We should teach math in schools for the same reasons we should teach visual art, music, poetry, and biology. Learning mathematics means studying topics such as algorithms, infinity, conjecturing, and proof.

I see these two reasons—practical skills and transmitting culture—as being quite different from more generalized claims about reasoning and problem-solving skills and certainly quite different from claims that mastering (for example) the quadratic formula will be useful later on. The honest answer for most students who ask when they will need to use the quadratic formula is "never." If we think the quadratic formula is important to teach, we should be ready to defend it as an artifact of culture—an example of an algorithm, perhaps.

An important part of the case I am building here is that my reasons invite conversation and debate about exactly what mathematics we should teach. On the side of utility, the portion of the mathematics curriculum that is useful changes over time in response to technological and cultural advances. Deriving by hand used to be the only way to find square roots accurate to an arbitrary number of digits. Now we have calculators. It used to be important for citizens to know the relationships of pecks to bushels. Now we more frequently buy and sell produce by the pound. The algorithm for deriving square roots with pencil and paper and relationships among outdated units of measure are examples of mathematics content that is no longer useful because of technological or cultural change.

It also makes sense to reflect on which aspects of math culture are important to hand down. Mathematical proof is an example. The logical certainty of proof is a different way of knowing than the experimental results of science or the metaphors of poetry (although to be sure, experimentation and metaphor each have important roles in mathematics). Having agreed that mathematical proof is an aspect of culture we wish to convey in schools, there are many ways to approach it, and these approaches are open to discussion and revision, unlike generalized appeals to reasoning skills or utility, which tend to accept the curriculum as it stands without critical examination.

Another aspect of my answer to *Why am I teaching this?* is a particular understanding of the nature of the discipline and its relationship to the subject we teach in school. I'll make these things explicit.

I used to think that *doing mathematics* meant asking and answering questions at the forefront of human knowledge. I thought that the only people who really did mathematics were research mathematicians—mostly at universities—and that this was pretty much inaccessible to me and to most of my students.

As I have studied the math learning of young children, I have come to understand that they are doing mathematics when they ask and answer questions at the forefront of their own knowledge. When children invent strategies, generalize, extend ideas, and build arguments, their activity is identical to that of a research mathematician. It makes no difference whether somebody else has previously thought these thoughts or derived these results. What matters is that they are new to the child.

A university mathematician, Peter Rejto, once told me a story of a four-year-old child who was asked, "Do you have more fingers on your left hand or your right hand?" This child looked at her hands and thought for a moment, then wordlessly touched the tips of the thumb and fingers on her right hand to those on her left hand. "In that moment," Peter concluded with delight, "she invented one-to-one correspondence!" *One-to-one correspondence* refers to the idea that two collections are the same size if you can find a way to match each object in one collection to one, and only one, object in the other collection. One-to-one correspondence is an essential idea to grasp (although not necessarily to name) when learning to count, and it leads to important ideas in higher mathematics, such as that there are exactly as many fractions as there are whole numbers, but that there are fewer fractions than there are numbers on the number line. This last result is credited to Georg Cantor, a nineteenth- and twentieth-century German mathematician who founded a branch of mathematics called set theory. The child in the story had the insight that she could compare the number of fingers on each hand without counting them. Cantor had the insight that he could compare infinite numbers of things without counting them. These are both mathematicians at work.

These moments of mathematical insight and creativity are common, not rare.

Educator and author Rafranz Davis has written about an experience her nephew Braeden had with the culture of school mathematics (Davis 2014). His second-grade class was studying symmetry, and Braeden was sure that—contrary to his teacher's claim—an ellipse such as the one on the left in Figure 2.1 does not have a line of symmetry running diagonally from upper left to lower right. The teacher and the class told him that he was wrong. Braeden—not to be defeated—rushed home at the end of the day to cut circles and ellipses out of paper and apply an important test of symmetry: He folded them in half. Recounting his inquiry to his aunt later that day, he proclaimed that he knew he was right because, when he folded along a diagonal line, "It looks like a messed up taco." Digging deeper, he diagnosed the reason that his teacher and classmates had gotten it wrong. "Maybe they were confused with congruence." The two halves of Braeden's messed-up taco have the same size and shape, but they are not reflections of each other. (See Figure 2.1.) There is more to a line of symmetry than cutting a shape into congruent halves. As Braeden said, "If you cut the oval in a diagonal and flip the pieces around, they are congruent. That's not the same as symmetry because you had to flip it."

Braeden is not the first mathematician to have his ideas rejected by the community, but his story is a stark reminder to us that a critical mind is an essential tool for seeking mathematical truth. Braeden was engaged in an important practice of

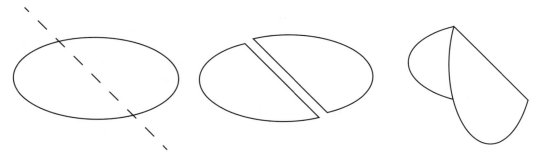

FIGURE 2.1
A line of symmetry requires more than congruent halves.

mathematicians. Yet this practice stood in contrast to perceived or actual practices of school mathematics. Braeden questioned an assumption—if we can cut a figure into two congruent halves with a straight line, then that line is a line of symmetry. Identifying and questioning assumptions that underlie definitions and claims is important and challenging mathematical work.

Chapter 4 is full of stories of children doing mathematics—the kind of mathematics that belongs in schools and which children pursue willingly, sometimes even defiantly. These children are motivated sometimes by curiosity, sometimes by pride, but not at all by an external promise of future utility.

HOW MANY?

How do children learn what it means to answer the question *How many?* Researcher Karen Fuson has described understanding numbers as having three components: *quantity*, *number language*, and *numeration* (Fuson et al. 1997). A simple but crude distinction among these three is the following:

- Quantity is how many things there are.

- Number language is how we say how many things there are.

- Numeration is how we write how many things there are.

For example, you know many ways of saying how many stars there are in Figure 2.2. *Two*, *a pair*, *dos*, and *a couple* are but a few of the possibilities here. Different people using these different expressions all agree, nonetheless, on how many stars there are. There are many different ways to express this quantity with number language. Similarly, you know several ways of writing this quantity. You could use our usual Hindu-Arabic numeration system (2), Roman numerals (II), or tally marks (//); these are all examples of different forms of numeration.

As an essential part of developing their understanding of numbers, children need to be able to move fluently among quantity, number language, and numeration, as in Figure 2.3. Viewed this way, "Put three of the apples on the table" is a different task

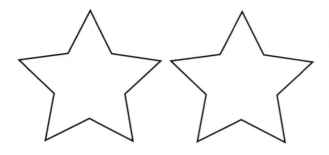

from asking a child to count three apples that are already on the table. The former task asks the child to go from number language to quantity. The latter task goes in the opposite direction, starting with a given quantity and asking the child to express it in language.

The following question demonstrates the complexity of the relationships among quantity, number language, and numeration: *How should we read the number 0.5 aloud?* Take a moment to consider multiple possibilities, and their pros and cons, before reading further.

First, I'll acknowledge that *should* is a loaded word. It implies that I'm seeking what is best or necessary, which varies, depending on the situation. Here are three possible responses; perhaps you will think of additional possibilities.

Zero point five. This is akin to spelling your name out loud. It can be useful for clear communication, but you lose the pronunciation, and you have to do a bit of mental work to recognize it and figure out how to pronounce it. When I want to be sure that my name is spelled correctly, I'll spell it for the listener. D-A-N-I-E-L-S-O-N, hitting the O with emphasis because that's where there is sometimes ambiguity. It is similar with long decimal representations. If I say *five one-millionths,* you'll likely have to work pretty hard to transcribe it properly. If I say *point zero-zero-zero* [pause] *zero-zero-five,* you'll get it right with little difficulty.

One half. This is a little bit like a nickname. There is no obvious connection between the expression in number language and the numeration we're looking at, just as I've never really understood why Margaret sometimes goes by Peggy. If I know Peggy well, I'll have no trouble substituting Margaret in formal written communication. Similarly,

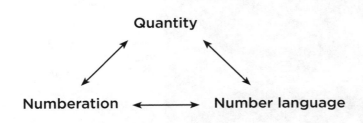

if I know the decimal and fraction systems of numeration well, I'll have no trouble recognizing 0.5 as one half. (Then again, how challenging is it to write the decimal equivalent for *one two-hundred-thousandth*? And what kind of work do you have to do in order to notice that it's the same as my earlier example, 0.000005?)

Five tenths. If I'm working with children who are still learning our decimal place value system, I prefer *five tenths* because it connects number language directly to numeration. Just like *five hundred* captures the digit and place value of 500 in words, so, too, does *five tenths* capture these things for 0.5.

The ideas of numeration, quantity, and number language capture what it means to learn how to count. But there are still lots of ways to get that count. That's what this next section is about: what are some ways of knowing how many things there are?

HOW DO YOU KNOW HOW MANY?

A story will illustrate the difference between saying how many things there are and saying how you know how many things there are. One day at Math On-A-Stick at the Minnesota State Fair, a four-year-old was counting the eggs in the picture in Figure 2.4 and got thirteen. Across the table, his ten-year-old sister was watching and shook her head in mild exasperation at the boy's conclusion.

I observed her disagreement and asked her how many there were. "Twelve," she said with confidence and a hint of disbelief that I needed to ask.

I asked how she knew and she said, "That's how they come." This may have been accompanied by an eye-roll too quick for me to see.

So I showed her the picture in Figure 2.5 and asked again how many. This time she

FIGURE 2.4
Twelve eggs

paused for a brief moment to think. "Twelve," she said with a small smirk. "How do you know?" I asked. "Because it's four rows of three," she said.

There are at least three ways of knowing how many—each displayed in this exchange. The ten-year-old was so familiar with cartons of eggs that she just knew that there were twelve. In recognizing quantity on sight, she *subitized.* This is the first way of knowing that I'll address next. Her four-year-old brother counted. This is the second way of knowing. Finally, when presented with an unfamiliar arrangement of eggs, my ten-year-old conversational partner used the structure of the carton to know—she saw four groups of three and knew that four groups of three is twelve. The use of number structure in this way is the third way of knowing how many.

Subitizing

Quantity is innate in human minds. We can notice numbers of things before we can walk, before we can talk, and before we can count. This may seem paradoxical, but it's true. It also seems like rather an impossible thing to study, so psychologists have had to design very clever experiments. In his terrific book *The Number Sense,* Stanislas Dehaene (2011) summarizes the relevant research with a variety of examples. In one such example, a baby sits in a parent's lap (and so feels safe and secure). The parent is blinded by a screen from seeing what the baby sees (and so cannot influence the results). Because babies look longer at surprising results or at things that are novel, the researchers track with great precision the amount of time the baby looks at what is going on. The researchers show the baby puppets going behind a curtain and then raise the curtain to reveal the puppets. When two puppets go behind the curtain and three puppets are revealed, the baby looks longer than when she sees the expected number of puppets. The baby notices that there is a different number of puppets than there should be. The conclusion is that—like color, shape, and pitch—quantity is a thing that babies can notice before they have words to express it.

This inborn ability to notice quantity without counting is called *subitizing*, and it is also inherent to most primates, many birds, and probably a bunch of other species, too. (Here again, knowing whether animals notice quantity takes careful research design.) If there are three eggs in the nest when a pigeon leaves and it returns to find only two, the pigeon will look for the third egg. This is evidence that the pigeon notices the quantity has changed. In all species, the ability to subitize seems to be limited to small numbers. In humans, that limit is four. Although adults can quickly identify five objects, studies of response times indicate that the time required is a bit greater than that required to identify four objects, while the time to identify four is the same as required to identify three. We recognize three and four at a glance; we must compute to know five. Consistent with this observation, a baby is not surprised when the six puppets that go behind the curtain are revealed as only five. Our

FIGURE 2.5
Twelve eggs in an unusual formation

innate number system seems to be limited to zero, one, two, three, four, and many.

There are at least two ways to build on this inborn number system: (1) identifying common structures and (2) estimating. When educators refer to *subitizing*, we are usually talking about training students to recognize arrangements of numbers rather than the strictly inborn number recognition. The baby's ability to recognize an incorrect number of puppets behind the curtain doesn't depend on their arrangement. My own ability to recognize that there are five pips on the die I just rolled (see Figure 2.6) does depend on their arrangement. That arrangement of five dots (which is called a *quincunx*) is a really useful thing to learn, though, and time spent on recognizing such common structures of numbers pays great dividends in using numbers to make sense of the world, as well as in expressing more abstract mathematical relationships. Routines such as number talks (see, e.g., Humphreys and Parker 2015; Parrish 2010) help children attend to these kinds of structures.

In elementary school arithmetic, ten-frames are a tool for learning to recognize particular arrangements of small numbers at a glance. A ten-frame is a diagram

consisting of a rectangle subdivided into two rows of five squares, as in Figure 2.7. Children generally interact with ten-frames by placing one counter per square to represent single-digit values or sums of single-digit numbers. A ten-frame representation can reveal properties of numbers that might be obscured by counting one at a time or working with unstructured groups. For example, the ten-frame in Figure 2.7 has eight counters and may support a child in noticing that eight is three more than five (because

FIGURE 2.6
A quincunx

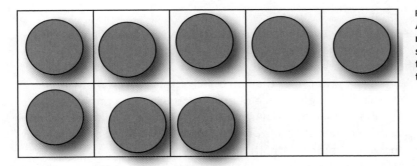

FIGURE 2.7
A ten-frame representing eight, and showing that eight is two less than ten but three more than five

the top row of five is filled and there are three more) and two less than ten (because there are two empty squares).

Familiarity with such relationships in turn supports robust mental math strategies. For example, 8 + 7 can be seen as three more than five, plus two more than five. The two fives are ten, the extra three and two make another five, so 8 + 7 = 15. Children who are offered lots of experiences with ten-frames and other structured representations of numbers tend to invent these kinds of strategies naturally. In this way, exploring various forms of subitizing can pay off as support for rich mathematical thinking.

Becoming familiar with common arrangements of quantities is one way to extend and build on our natural ability to identify quantities without counting. Another way is to practice estimating large quantities. In recent years, neuroscientists have begun to study our ability to tell the difference between 100 and 1,000 objects at a glance. Researchers have found that the brain's so-called *approximate number system* (or ANS) is (a) trainable (Park and Brannon 2013) and (b) tied to success in school mathematics (Halberda, Mazzocco, and Feigenson 2008). In short, children who are better at estimating large numbers of objects tend to be more successful in math later on, and children get better at this kind of estimation with practice.

Counting

Recognizing quantities—whether by evolutionary subitizing, pattern identification, or estimation—is one way of knowing how many. Counting is another.

When my son was about two years old, my father—who lives a good distance away, and whom we see several times a year rather than on a daily basis—asked me whether Griffin knew how to count. This seemingly simple question actually has a rather complicated answer. I'll provide a quick overview here of what it means to know how to count, and I'll recommend the wonderful book *Young Children's Mathematics* (Carpenter et al. 2016) for readers who want a more in-depth discussion.

Learning to count involves coordinating multiple skills. Three big ideas to be mastered and related to one another are *one-to-one correspondence, cardinality,* and *the counting sequence.* At a formal level, one-to-one correspondence is the idea that two sets are the same size if you can find a way to match up each item in one set with exactly one item in the other set and have no unmatched leftovers in either set. On a snowy school day, there ought to be a one-to-one correspondence between the feet of kindergartners and the child-sized boots in the cubby area. There is not a one-to-one correspondence between kindergartners and boots, as you need two boots per kindergartner.

Cardinality is quantity. Understanding cardinality refers to knowing that the last number you say when counting a set is the quantity of the things in the set. It is not uncommon for young children to correctly count each of the eight objects and then, when asked "How many are there?" to give an incorrect response such as *five* or to take the question as a command to count again. The understanding that saying *eight* on the final object is making a claim about the set as a whole is its own achievement—related to, but independent of, the other counting skills. Another important aspect of cardinality being a property of a set is that order and organization do not affect it. If you count the objects in a different order (left to right instead of right to left, or even in an arbitrary order), the total number is unchanged. If you rearrange the objects by putting them in a line or an array or an unorganized heap, their total number is unchanged.

To talk about this distinction, mathematicians and math educators refer to *cardinal numbers* and *ordinal numbers.* Cardinal numbers indicate the size of a set. Ordinal numbers are like names assigned to individual items in the set. When a child counts a set of eight objects, she assigns the name *one* to the first object, *two* to the second object, and so on, up to assigning the name *eight* to the eighth object. One-to-one correspondence assures that she gives each object exactly one name. At the end of the counting process, *eight* needs to also take on a second meaning—it is not just the name of the last object she counted, it also states the size of the set. Eight needs to take on the role of a cardinal number.

The book *Children's Mathematics* (Carpenter et al. 2014) reports results from the Cognitively Guided Instruction (CGI) research project at the University of Wisconsin–Madison. The premise of the project is that young children come to school with powerful mathematical ideas but that these ideas may differ from an adult's way of thinking. When teachers better understand their students' ideas, they have a better basis for making instructional decisions, and children learn more as a result. CGI set out to document the ways students think about addition and subtraction problems, to associate these ways of thinking with strategies students use to solve problems, and to study how teachers who know these ways of thinking interact with and support their students. One of the videos accompanying the first edition of the book offers a wonderful example of a boy solving a subtraction problem by counting.

Here is the problem he solves in the video: Abubu had ten stickers. He lost three of them. How many stickers does he have left? The standard technique for solving this problem by counting is to say the following, "He had ten stickers. Nine, eight, seven. He has seven stickers left." The boy in the video speaks slightly different words: "He had ten stickers. Ten, nine, eight. Take away that; it's seven."

When I use this video in a math course for future elementary teachers, my students initially interpret the boy's words "take away that; it's seven" as a correction. In this view, he knows that 10 − 3 is 7, but he makes an error when telling the interviewer how he solved the problem. So he corrects that error at the end. While this is certainly possible, a more likely explanation is that these words accurately represent his thinking. In this view, his counting is a recitation of ordinal numbers rather than cardinal numbers.

In the standard technique for counting back, we say *nine* when there are nine objects remaining, *eight* when eight objects remain, and *seven* at the end. At each step, the numbers we say represent the cardinality of the remaining set. In the video, the boy says *ten* when he takes away object number ten, *nine* when he removes object number nine, and *eight* when he removes object number eight. "Take that [the eighth one] away; it's seven," he says. This is a child with a strong understanding of the relationship between ordinal and cardinal numbers (although, at about eight years old, he probably doesn't know these terms). If the same boy had been counting to solve an addition problem such as 5 + 3, we would not have evidence of his knowledge of this relationship. When a child says *six, seven, eight*, we have no way to know whether she is thinking about ordinal numbers (the sixth, the seventh, and the eighth objects) or cardinal numbers (now there are six objects; now there are seven objects; now there are eight). These differences are subtle, but misunderstanding a child's thinking can mean the difference between supporting his correct but unconventional work and undermining it by telling him it's wrong.

A student of mine, and future elementary teacher, once referred to the counting sequence as *the number poem*. This is a useful way of thinking about learning number words. There is rhyme and rhythm in the ordered words of the number poem, which is apparent if you've ever been in a classroom of primary-grade children engaged in choral counting. *Twenty-eight, twenty-niiiiiiiine . . . thirty.* The drawn-out nine and the emphasis on thirty help children to identify and use the repeating structure of English number language.

The number poem contains within it many other number poems.

- *Two, four, six, eight . . .*

- *One, three, five, seven, nine . . .*

- *Three, six, nine, twelve, fifteen, eighteen . . .*

These skip-counting sequences support more efficient counting techniques. If you have to go past eighteen and nineteen every time you count twenty things, you experience

FIGURE 2.8
Wooden tiling turtles

the pain of inefficiency. You're more likely to lose track of your count and need to start over. You're also more likely to make mistakes and get different answers for two different counts of the same set. You're going to be overwhelmed by large collections and may choose not to count them. But if you know some skip-counting number poems, and if you can see or create structures in the things you are counting, your counting will be more accurate and faster.

For example, I make wooden tiling turtles on a laser cutter, and package them for sale in sets of twenty-five—typically thirteen light turtles and twelve dark ones or vice versa (Figure 2.8). If I try to count sets of thirteen or twelve individually, I get it wrong about 17 percent of the time. Worse, if I think I may have gotten my count wrong, I have to recount from the beginning. I can't tell thirteen from twelve (or even from eleven) at a glance. So now I put them in piles of five, which I can subitize. Once all of the light-colored turtles are in piles of five, I take three turtles and two piles to make each set of thirteen. From an unorganized heap of turtles, I create structure (groups of five) and then use a more efficient skip-counting strategy (*five, ten, thirteen*) for faster, more accurate results.

Multiplicative structure

Counting and its various forms—counting on, counting back, skip counting—exploit an additive structure of numbers. Numbers also have a multiplicative structure, which is about groups. When the ten-year-old egg counter at the fair told me there were twelve

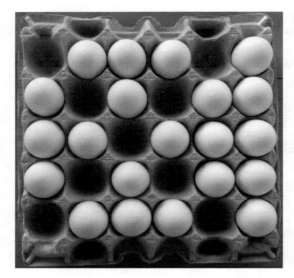

FIGURE 2.9
How can groups help you count the eggs?

eggs because she saw four rows of three, she was referring to the multiplicative structure of twelve.

One way to think about the meaning of multiplication is that A x B means A groups of B. Eggs usually come in two groups of six and sometimes in three groups of four. When you are using multiplication as a structure for counting, you look for same-sized groups. Try this out on Figure 2.9. Count the eggs by looking for same-sized groups before reading further.

One way of counting these eggs is to count the number in each row. If you use the additive structure of the eggs, you'll add 4 + 4 + 5 + 4 + 4. If you use the multiplication structure, you'll say it's four groups of four, and five more. The difference between these two structures is subtle, and it can take time to learn to appreciate it. Multiplicative structure is essential to later learning about fractions, area, and algebra. It's worth the time and effort to learn to use it as a central part of teaching at a wide range of grade levels.

When a student is trying to figure out the product 3 x 6, asking about three groups of six allows you and the student to build a connection to three groups of five, which is a product many children find easier to recall or to quickly reconstruct than 3 x 6. The idea that three groups of six must be three more than three groups of five is simpler than knowing that 6 + 6 + 6 is three more than 5 + 5 + 5, because there are fewer things to keep track of. Attending to multiplicative structures while counting often requires less mental effort, and it supports building relationships—a recurring theme throughout this book. Similarly, a student who doesn't know what five groups of eight is can benefit from thinking about ten groups of eight or about eight groups of five. This kind of thinking is more accessible when you're thinking about multiplicative structure rather than additive structure.

WHAT ARE YOU COUNTING?

Minneapolis high school teacher Sara Van Der Werf has a bulletin board in her classroom titled "Math Fails" that is filled with photographs of real-world math gone wrong. Nissan sells a car called the "Cube" that is not actually a cube; McDonald's has cups that say "half full > half empty," etc. She uses these images to spark conversation among her students. There is humor, a bit of "look what you students can do that adults cannot," and a dash of "Mistakes happen; let's notice them, shake them off, and move on." She documents and shares her Math Fails on her blog: saravanderwerf.com.

A while back, I began capturing my favorite genre of Math Fails under the hashtag #unitchat. It is remarkable how often we get the digits right but in the wrong places. Consider Figure 2.10. It is probably clear to everyone reading this sign that the restaurant is not actually offering a hundred-dollar sandwich, but without the decimal point, that's how it reads. Now look at the gas station sign in Figure 2.11. This time, the sign doesn't tell us the units so we are free to infer them. If unleaded costs 317 somethings per gallon, that something must be *cents*. At the time I took this photo, 317 cents was a perfectly reasonable

FIGURE 2.10
If the sign is correct, this is a very expensive sandwich.

FIGURE 2.11
Are the units consistent on this sign?

price for a gallon of gas. Notice that diesel is similarly priced, so the units are consistent. But this consistency makes the discount offered on line 3 negligible. Three one-hundredths of *what*? A penny? No thanks; not worth my time. In fact, 0.03 cents wouldn't even change the fraction in the photograph if they round to the nearest tenth of a cent.

These are common oversights and errors. Where #unitchat started to get complicated was when I noticed that units are sometimes used deliberately to manipulate shoppers' minds. Figure 2.12 is strong evidence that consumer paper products are badly in need of regulation. Anticipating the possibility of government intervention, lawsuits, or both, these manufacturers specify their units in teeny-tiny type beneath each number—Mega Rolls or Big Rolls are being compared to Regular Rolls, and even then Regular Rolls are defined elsewhere with an asterisk. Pity the shopper who has been dispatched by a spouse to buy a dozen rolls of toilet paper.

Over time, #unitchat has evolved. I am now less interested in capturing mistakes than in finding ambiguity. An ideal #unitchat image has multiple things to count, as well as multiple units for counting them: shoes and pairs of shoes, pizzas and slices of pizza, avocados and half-avocados. These are instances of moving from right and wrong to nuance and depth. I still love a good math fail, of course. But for training young minds to think deeply about numerical relationships, I have come to understand the power of a prompt that supports multiple ways of thinking.

FIGURE 2.12
What a tangled web we weave when we use units to deceive.

Place value

Units and groups are the essence of place value. Thinking of 130 as thirteen tens, 1.3 hundreds, or as 1,300 tenths is the foundation for deeper understanding of the algorithms of arithmetic and of algebraic representations of numbers.

When students learn place value from the perspective of naming places they are ill-equipped to understand algorithms with meaning. Randy Philipp and his research team have written about a question they call "The Ones Task," which illustrates this (Philipp 2008). In the standard addition and subtraction algorithms taught in most American elementary schools, you can end up writing a little "1" above the tens place, as in the two examples in Figure 2.13. The Ones Task asks about the precise meaning of each of these ones. Philipp's research team used The Ones Task with preservice elementary teachers and has found that this population struggles to state that the 1 in the subtraction algorithm represents one group of 100, while the 1 in the addition algorithm represents one group of ten. Without this understanding, the standard algorithms for addition and subtraction lack meaning. Why do we treat this part of the addition algorithm as six, and the corresponding part of the subtraction algorithm as fifteen? The answer to that question is rooted in the meanings of the respective 1s.

The two 1s in The Ones Task count different units, and keeping track of shifting units is essential to understanding place value. In Chapter 4, I go into the idea of shifting units in place value in depth by telling the story of a profound insight my daughter

$$\begin{array}{r} {}^{3}\!\not{4}\,{}^{1}59 \\ -84 \\ \hline 375 \end{array} \qquad\qquad \begin{array}{r} 2\,{}^{1}57 \\ +35 \\ \hline 292 \end{array}$$

FIGURE 2.13
The Ones Task: What is the meaning of the little "1" in each calculation?

once had on a stormy summer evening: "Asking 'How many tens are in thirty?' is like asking 'How many ones are in two?'"

In this chapter, I have touched on several big ideas that children encounter as they learn to count, and I have argued that learning to count is a more challenging—and far more interesting—endeavor than it may appear to a casual observer of children's mathematical activity. These big ideas form the mathematical structure of *How Many?* In the next chapter, I'll help you think about the classroom and conversational structures that you'll need in order to make *How Many?* conversations productive for you and your students.

CHAPTER 3

How to Use *How Many?* in Your Classroom

A fter visiting many classrooms to probe children's ideas about geometry while I worked on the first book in this series, *Which One Doesn't Belong?* I began to play with similar ways of inviting children into conversations about counting and units. Yet there was a lingering worry in the back of my mind—maybe geometry is special. "Maybe geometry is a topic that allows children to explore and play and conjecture in response to an open, ambiguous question," a voice in the back of my head kept saying, "Maybe counting doesn't offer the same opportunities."

Of course, I knew this worry was silly. In fact, just a few years earlier I was harboring the opposite concern. I loved teaching place value and fractions in my math courses for preservice elementary teachers, but I dreaded the work in geometry. However, I have learned that dread about teaching a math topic is usually a sign that I haven't studied the topic carefully enough. *Which One Doesn't Belong?* taught me that geometry is about relationships, not vocabulary and formally structured proofs. *How Many?* was about to teach me that counting is also about relationships.

By the time I had assembled a workable draft of the student book, I had mostly quieted that skeptical voice. Conversations in my home, with my adult math students, and with my colleagues and editor had all served to reassure me that carefully considered images could provoke rich ideas about counting and units. So I entered a first-grade classroom genuinely curious—if still a bit uncertain—about what children would see, what they would say, and what math we would do together.

We are going to look at some pictures together. Each time, I'll ask you the same question, "How many?" and I'll be interested to hear your answers.

When I ask "How many?" if you think "How many what?" then you have the idea. In each picture, there are lots of things you could count. So you won't want to just say "one," you'll need to tell us what you see one of.

It didn't take long. Those first graders were eager to share the things that they saw, to build off of one another's ideas, to learn new words, and to think new thoughts. My concerns about the content—counting versus geometry—quickly proved unfounded. It hadn't been geometry per se driving the inquiry in *Which One Doesn't Belong?,* it had been the interactions among an engaging image; a simple, open question; and the curious, creative minds of children.

WHAT IS A *HOW MANY?* CONVERSATION?

A *How Many?* conversation may take place in three minutes or thirty. It may involve a parent and child snuggled on a couch in the evening, a small group of first graders at choice time, a teacher and twenty-five third graders launching their day's mathematical activity, or any of a thousand other combinations of people. Each of these contexts has in common that the participants are on equal footing and that they are looking for structure.

Equal Footing

In a *How Many?* conversation, all participants have equal access to the mathematics. It is not a quiz in which the answers are predetermined and held secret by the teacher. It is not a game of *I Spy* in which a particular response is the target and—once uttered— ends the game. In a genuine *How Many?* conversation, the mathematics exists in the interactions among the participants, provoked by the image. As a teacher (and as a reader of this book!) you have expertise that informs your judgment about what mathematics your students are likely to see. You should use that expertise to make sure important mathematics happens in the group. At the same time, you need to make sure that everyone understands that the math comes from the participants, not from an answer key, a standards document, or some other place of authority.

Looking for Structure

The participants in a *How Many?* conversation look for and discuss relationships, commonalities, and differences in each image and across images. If someone says they see twelve eggs, either they will volunteer how they know there are twelve eggs or someone will be likely to ask about it.

An important role—often, but not always, played by the teacher—is of pressing for clarity. "I counted" is a vague but common answer to the question, "How do you know there are twelve eggs?" There are several ways to press for clarity in such a claim. Asking "Did you say the number eleven in your head as you counted?" is one example. If the student says "No," then "How *did* you count?" is a follow-up question that will help the student understand how to answer meaningfully. Counting by twos, or by threes, or noticing that there are three rows of four are all possible, different strategies that could be hidden beneath "I counted," and each highlights an important mathematical structure of the sort that *How Many?* is designed to bring out.

Indeed, part of what students learn from *How Many?* conversations is what it means to say how you counted. Like dot-image number talks (see Humphreys and Parker 2015), *How Many?* conversations are about learning to see and express structure. The abstract dots of a number talk focus students' attention on multiple structures for the same count. The image at the focus of a *How Many?* conversation is usually less richly structured for any one count but opens up a wide range of possible counts and relationships among them—including messy and imagined relationships such as the number of people who could share fifteen half-avocados' worth of guacamole, or the fate of the missing half-avocado.

A *How Many?* conversation puts the participants on equal footing and focuses everyone's attention on mathematical structure. The next section will help you develop techniques for making this happen in your classroom.

THE PEDAGOGY OF *HOW MANY?*

My home has many cookbooks. One of these was on the breakfast table one morning, an artifact of the previous evening's last-minute meal planning: *5 Ingredients or Less! Dump Meals.* My children—Tabitha (who is ten years old) and Griffin (who is thirteen)—and I discussed the relative merits of the book and of the meals we had eaten that came from its recipes. There was some disagreement on these things (mostly good-natured), but Tabitha put her foot down on one matter. "They all have more than five ingredients," she sighed with impatience.

My experience with *How Many?* conversations—in classrooms and outside of them—made me sit up and take notice, for here was an opportunity to investigate a counting claim. "It's in big letters on the cover—part of the title in fact! It's got to be true!" I countered.

"Nope," Tabitha shook her head. "Go ahead and look."

So we cracked open the book. The first recipe we looked at had the following ingredients:

Pinto beans

Black beans

Diced tomatoes

Salsa

Frozen corn

Minced onion

Chili powder

Ground cumin

Sour cream (optional)

Shredded Cheddar cheese (optional)

I turned the page—eight ingredients in that recipe, and the next one had six. "See?" Tabitha said with a certain amount of smugness.

"There must be a place where they say what counts as an ingredient," I said as I flipped pages to begin my search. Sure enough, in a sidebar about the usefulness of a well-stocked pantry, I found this passage: "[This book] features recipes that can be created with 5 ingredients and/or the addition of these common pantry items," followed by a list of such things as milk, eggs, oil, onions, spices, and flour. Arguably, each of the ten items listed in the first recipe that Tabitha, Griffin, and I considered could be in a well-stocked pantry, so it's really unclear why these recipes need any ingredients at all! Why not go all the way and advertise a zero-ingredient cookbook?

The *Dump Meals* story has a small addendum. The back cover summarizes the book's premise this way: "Toss 5 ingredients or less into your slow cooker and have dinner ready in no time!" This version of the claim is quite a bit harder to swallow. Pinto beans count as an ingredient but onions don't because I am supposed to have onions in my pantry. Am I also supposed to have them in my slow cooker? Do they mince themselves? Even the most generous interpretation of this claim stops here. Tabitha was right.

This brief morning conversation illustrates several important principles to keep in mind as you think about using *How Many?* with learners. I'll expand on each of these in the next section.

- Tell stories

- Seek to understand and to be understood

- Insist only on necessary precision

- Develop expertise

A *How Many?* conversation is an opportunity to bring children and mathematics together in a way that feels different from more tightly structured curricular materials.

But rich mathematical discourse doesn't just happen because you've put away the worksheets. There are some basic principles to keep in mind, and some concrete steps you can take to support the kind of mathematical activity you're hoping to inspire in your classroom.

Tell Stories

When my children were very young, we read picture books with rich and interesting characters taking on complicated and challenging situations. We were especially fond of Russell Hoban's classic *Bread and Jam for Frances* (1964), in which Frances—an early-elementary-aged anthropomorphic badger—declares that the only food she likes is bread with jam. Her exasperated family indulges this demand, and (spoiler alert!) over the course of several days, Frances tires of the monotony, relents, and begins to delight in a richly varied diet. My children and I could relate to Frances and her disgust with a jiggly soft-boiled egg at the book's outset. Indeed, I can vividly recall a time when one of my own children declared an entire slice of watermelon inedible because of a supposedly mushy bit where a seed had been. For the record, there was no mushy bit; there could not have been a mushy bit because there is no watermelon in an empty space! But I digress. The point is that we understood our lives a bit differently through this book, and we understood the book a bit differently for having lived our lives together. After reading a favorite storybook, we would pick up a shapes book or a numbers book and have a much less engrossing experience. Triangles, then squares, then rectangles on the next page (but never a square on the rectangle page!). One of this, two of that, three of another. These math-focused books were much less likely to resonate with us after the book was finished and offered many fewer opportunities for us to bring our experience to bear on the books' content.

How Many? (and its sibling book *Which One Doesn't Belong?*) aims to break this cycle, because math has stories, too. I hope you and your students will recognize their life experiences here and recognize the ideas of the book in their lives. I hope you will have some students who have never tried avocado and that other students will have stories to tell about making guacamole with a family member. I hope grapefruit juice will provoke a reaction in some children just as a soft-boiled egg did in Frances.

In the classroom, this hope means leaving a bit of space for storytelling. Tell your own stories, and invite the children in your classroom to share their experiences with buying shoes or cutting pizza. Let your students be the experts for a while, and share your expertise as well. Laugh together. Empathize. Here is how this looks when I visit classrooms:

"Here's an interesting object (Figure 3.1). Raise your hand if you know what this is," I ask of the class. The fraction of the class that responds varies greatly here. Pretty much every class has at least a few students who recognize avocados, and pretty much every class has at least a couple of students who do not.

I generally pick a student to share. "Please tell us what this thing is called and a little bit of what you know about it." We hear the word *avocado*, which I repeat slowly because I know it is new for some students in the room, and more importantly we hear about parents and grandparents, family dinners, restaurants, grocery stores, vacations, and even the occasional kitchen accident. I ask the children who know what avocados are whether they like avocados, and these children are never unanimous—but always opinionated—on the yumminess of avocados in many forms. Usually someone talks about how they once grew a large houseplant from the pit of an avocado. I live in Minnesota, so no one talks about avocado trees in their yard or neighborhood, but surely they would if I visited classrooms in warmer climes. I usually tell the students about my friend Sam, who likes to cut his avocados in half and fill their indentations with balsamic vinegar.

FIGURE 3.1
Avocados provide opportunities for storytelling.

After a few minutes of sharing our stories, everyone in the room has enough context to understand what they're looking at and enough words to describe what they see to someone else. If these students are new to *How Many?* I initiate them. If they are familiar with it, we move right into the conversation about numbers and units. The stories get us started; they connect us to the math and to one another. They provide a context for considering mathematical relationships (such as wondering how many delicious balsamic-filled avocado halves my friend Sam can get from a bag full of avocados).

Seek to Understand and to Be Understood

When we were looking at *Dump Meals* together, Tabitha and I didn't stay at the surface of our disagreement for long. She said the recipes had more than five ingredients; I said they couldn't have more than five ingredients; she said to look inside the book. Evidence plays a crucial role in seeking to understand and to be understood. Tabitha insisted I consider evidence rather than just what *should* be. I wanted to find evidence of what the author considered an ingredient.

One of the things people appreciate about mathematics is that many disagreements can be resolved through improved understanding of an alternate perspective. Recently, teacher and mother Sara McGee shared the following claim from her nine-year-old daughter: "I think there might not really be any prime numbers." Sara's response was to ask her daughter to say more. Her daughter offered twenty-three as an example and said that—in addition to 23 x 1—you can factor twenty-three as $11\frac{1}{2}$ times 2, and, furthermore, you can do that with any number at all. Therefore, there are no prime numbers. This is exactly the sort of thing that mathematicians resolve through careful understanding. When we talk about prime numbers, we usually mean to define them in terms of whole-number factors. Number theorists and algebraists would say that twenty-three is prime *over the natural numbers*. If you allow fractions, however, then all numbers have lots of factors, and so twenty-three is not prime *over the rational numbers*. Whether twenty-three is prime depends on what counts as a factor, just as whether *Dump Meals* recipes contain at most five ingredients depends on what counts as an ingredient.

This sort of clarifying question about what counts comes up frequently in *How Many?* conversations. If we're counting toppings in the pizza pictures, does *cheese* count as a topping? If you say yes, there are four toppings. If you say no, there are three. When students disagree about the number of toppings, check whether they agree on what counts as a topping. If this process is new to your students—if they are accustomed to definitions being imposed by external authorities, say—it may take some time for them to become comfortable living in the ambiguity of multiple ways of viewing a counting situation. But it is worth the time invested; an enriched and nuanced worldview is a noble aim of education.

Insist Only on Necessary Precision

Not all precision in mathematics is necessary. Consider the example of fractions. A fully precise, mathematically correct definition of a fraction is this:

> *A fraction is an equivalence class of ordered pairs of integers (a, b), with b ≠ 0, such that (a, b) is equivalent to (c, d) if and only if ad = bc.*

Wrestling with this definition is a standard part of an undergraduate course in abstract algebra, where it is necessary because abstract algebra is a place for asking and answering deep, sometimes philosophical, questions about the nature of numbers and operations. In that context, this level of precision is necessary. When fourth graders are thinking about how to share four small pizzas equally among seven people, this level of precision is not necessary.

In mathematics in general, and in a *How Many?* conversation in particular, it is best to insist only on *necessary* precision rather than on precision for precision's sake. Most cookbooks don't need to be precise about what counts as an ingredient because they don't make claims about the number of ingredients in the recipes. Likewise, there is no reason to begin conversations about the pizza images in *How Many?* by asking whether cheese counts as a topping. The need for a precise meaning of *pizza topping* arises when there is disagreement about the number of toppings.

There may be times when you want your students to practice the skill of using precise language, but all of your students agree on the number of toppings on those pizzas. In such a case, you can take a contrary position in order to force your students to defend theirs and to define *pizza topping* along the way. You may also assign such contrary positions to last year's students (possibly fictional), acquaintances, or even to this book's author. (So long as you give me a heads-up by e-mail, I will gladly claim to have any understanding of pizza toppings that will advance noble educational goals in your classroom.)

DEVELOP EXPERTISE

I once attended an arts integration workshop led by Malke Rosenfeld. Malke's work is in the overlap of mathematics and percussive dance. At the beginning of the workshop, she did two short demonstration dances of between five and ten seconds each, and then asked us, "Which one of those makes sense?" I had to admit that neither one made any sense to me and that I would have been hard-pressed to express many characteristics of either one. To Malke (and possibly any number of my coparticipants in the workshop), her first demonstration dance was arbitrary and unstructured, while the second was a structured and familiar pattern.

I was struck by these different perspectives on the same phenomenon, and I wondered whether a similar kind of difference occurs whenever novices and experts encounter content together. I thought of times when I've looked at a challenging algebra problem with my students and I have seen structures in the problem that they have not. From that experience, I have begun to think of this difference in perception as a key difference between novices and experts. A novice has trouble separating signal from noise. As a novice to percussive dance, I couldn't tell which of Malke's dances was supposed to make sense and which was not because I couldn't tell what mattered. I couldn't distinguish the signal from the noise. Similarly, my algebra students haven't learned to tell which features of an algebra problem matter and which do not.

This distinction between novices and experts helps me think about goals for learners and can inform the ways we work with *How Many?* We want our learners to develop into experts, and this means giving them time to explore and to experiment. It also means that we don't expect expertise at the outset. You can expect it to take time for your students to notice the mathematics of units and unit relationships in their own lives, to get really good at carefully explaining their ideas in order to be understood, and to use precise language without prompting. Keep the end goal in mind. Be patient and persistent.

I recently tested my own developing expertise in answering *How Many?* when I wrote the answers that are in Chapter 5. I set myself the challenge of finding something I had not designed into the book from the beginning (Note to self: Design this into the next book from the beginning!), namely, a sequence of answers that started with one thing in the first image, two things in the second image, three things in the third, and so on throughout the book. If you try this yourself, or if you read this part of Chapter 5, you will see that this task is challenging. I might not have been successful before my own experiences with *How Many?*

WHAT MATH IS IN A *HOW MANY?* CONVERSATION?

In Chapter 2, I discussed how children learn to count. In this section, I'll say more about the ways in which *How Many?* conversations can support this learning.

Noticing Structure

One of the most productive mathematics questions is, "How do you know?" Asking, "How do you know?" is different from asking, "Why?" because the former question is personal, and the teacher cannot know its answer in advance. "Why?" is also a great question but is more likely to be tied to a predetermined explanation. "How do you know?" asks about the child's thinking process, which in most cases the child knows a lot about. "Why?" asks for a justification that a child may not have any insight about at all.

The various answers to the question, "How do you know?" that arise in a classroom expose mathematical structure for everyone to examine. Consider the avocado array in Figure 3.2. If everyone agrees that there are seven and one-half avocados and the class moves on, an opportunity to notice structure has been missed. Here are three possible answers to the follow-up question, "How do you know?"

- I counted fifteen half-avocados and then divided that by two.

- I matched the avocado halves in order to make whole avocados. I could do that seven times, with one half left over.

- There are eight empty spaces, so there must have been eight pits that came from eight avocados. There are only seven pits. Therefore, we are missing a half-avocado with a pit.

The first two strategies use division, and the teacher can help students notice this common structure by asking about it. "How are these two strategies alike?" can lead students to notice that making groups of two is related to dividing by two. The third strategy, by contrast, involves one-to-one correspondence rather than division. Each avocado has one pit, so counting pits is a proxy for counting avocados. Asking, "How do you know?" brings these two structures—division and one-to-one correspondence—into the open and makes them available to learn and use in the future.

Identifying Units

We don't pay much attention to units in most math teaching. We tend to be so interested in the numbers (or variables) and their properties that many problems involving units exist only to highlight these properties. A 4-by-6 rectangle might be 4 mm by 6 mm and smaller than your thumbnail, or it might be 4 miles by 6 miles and larger than an airport. The way you work with these very different objects is mathematically the same—multiply the values to find their areas, for example—but when the problems stem from our lived experiences, the units matter very much. If I'm buying a rug for my living room, a 4-foot-by-6-foot rug will function very differently from a 4-meter-by-6-meter one.

This devaluing of units isn't limited

FIGURE 3.2
The avocado array is an important place to ask, "How do you know how many?"

FIGURE 3.3
How many?

to story problems in school; it can be found in many counting books as well. A typical counting book begins with one dog, then two cats on the next page, and three birds after that. Why one dog, but two cats? It could just as easily be one cat and then two dogs. The units don't matter and can substitute for each other without changing the mathematical relationships.

How Many? conversations put the units front and center. When a student recently said she saw three dividers in the photo in Figure 3.3, a discussion ensued about whether she meant *vertical* dividers or *horizontal* dividers and about whether there were three of each type (running from edge to edge of the display) or twelve of each type (running from edge to edge of each of the sixteen cells in the display). The units matter here because they clarify the thing that you're counting. The units help us to understand one another better, and they open new questions. The units also matter because one unit determines the other, which I'll discuss in the next section.

Unit Relationships

The sixteen cells, three vertical dividers, and three horizontal dividers in Figure 3.3 are connected to one another. There are sixteen cells *because* there are three vertical and three horizontal dividers. This is an example of a relationship between units. Another relationship is that there are thirty-two lenses in sixteen pairs of glasses. (The musician Prince once designed eyeglasses with a third lens between and a bit above the usual two; seeing them on display in an eyeglass shop is a very strange life goal of mine.)

Attending to the relationships between units is important work for understanding place value, where tens, hundreds, thousands, and so on are units with a common relationship involving factors of ten. It is also important work for developing multiplicative reasoning because multiplication changes units. When you find area, you multiply two measurements in linear units (such as inches or meters) and get an area in square units (square inches or square meters). If you ride your bicycle at eight miles per hour for two hours, you ride sixteen miles. Each of these three numbers has different units, but those units have a relationship that can be obscured when the multiplication takes place in a context where the units are window dressing for fact practice. *How Many?* conversations can put these relationships front and center for examination and discussion.

Questioning Assumptions

Earlier, I wrote about the one-to-one correspondence between pits and avocados. It is such a safe assumption that each avocado has one pit that it doesn't seem worth questioning. But you could. And if you do, the direct evidence in the avocado array leads you to the same conclusion—there are still seven and one-half avocados. This can be a second role of the question "How do you know?" To avoid annoying children with repetition, here are some variants.

- Are you sure?

- Is that always true?

- How could we check?

- Do we *know* that?

- Does it have to be that way?

Every assumption can be tested by this sort of questioning. Early in the process, you may need to ask the questions. Over time, your students will learn to do it, too.

FIGURE 3.4
A double-yolked egg

The goal is to create a habit of keeping mathematical claims close to the evidence at hand.

An example of why questioning assumptions is important is the double-yolked egg in Figure 3.4. If you assume that each egg has one yolk, then you'll count five fried eggs. If you assume that all of the eggs in the pan have come from the carton, then you'll count four fried eggs, and one of them must have two yolks. The eggshells provide confirming evidence of four eggs. And now I need to tell you a little secret, which I hope you'll be able to keep. Stenhouse hired a magnificent photographer (Scott Dorrance) and food stylist (Lorie Dorrance) to produce the images in the student book. When people were concerned about the difficulty of my desire for a double-yolked egg in this image, Lorie declared that making a double-yolked egg is one of the simpler illusions in the profession. The true story of this double-yolked egg is that the second yolk came from another egg whose white and shell have been whisked away from the scene. Don't tell anyone, OK?

A few years ago, some online colleagues and I had fun questioning assumptions about pizza slices. We had been thinking about when and how decimals are introduced to students in a formal way in school. In particular, my question was, "Is there anything in a child's life that routinely gets cut into ten pieces?" because if we introduce decimals before common fractions in school, tenths are the first fractions they encounter. My colleagues suggested pizza.

You *can* slice a pizza into ten slices, but I questioned whether anybody ever had. So we began a search. We found a video (http://tinyurl.com/10slicepizza) in which a chef tells us to make a slice all the way across, then rotate the pizza at a 36° angle (which he does not measure). He rotates and slices the pizza three times, yielding four cuts and eight slices total (which he does not count) and announces that his task is complete.

This story is filled with assumptions—all of which need questioning. The first is that understanding decimals depends only on understanding whole-number place value, rather than also depending on a deep understanding of fractions. Another is that because pizzas are sliced in real life, we can use them to build understanding of fractions with arbitrary denominators. Finally, there is the perfectly reasonable assumption that when a chef tells us he is going to cut a pizza into ten slices, he will actually do so. Questioning assumptions requires a critical eye. I hope *How Many?* helps your students to be critical consumers of mathematical claims.

HOW TO TALK ABOUT *HOW MANY?*

Like *Which One Doesn't Belong?*—the first book in this series—*How Many?* isn't a textbook or a unit of study. It is closer to a storybook than a math text, so any of the ways that you might use a favorite picture book can be adapted for *How Many?*

Whole Group

Before having students turn and talk in pairs or small groups, do some counting together in a large group. This way you can model your expectations. Here are a few things you'll want to include in your instructions:

- Wait time. Students need to give one another time to think. This means no waving hands in the air and no talking until a given amount of time has passed. You know your students and their needs, but about a minute is a good amount of thinking time for getting a *How Many?* conversation started.

- Clear statements of units. Every answer to the question "how many?" includes both a number and a unit. Simply saying "four" doesn't tell us what you counted. Similarly, "shoelaces" tells us what you counted, but not how many you see.

Familiarize your students with the routines of pausing for thought and stating both a number and a unit. Then you can have them talk in small groups or pairs, or use whatever structures you have in place for breaking conversations into manageable-sized pieces so everyone can have a turn in a small amount of time.

Here are a couple of fun variations you might consider after you and your students have a bit of experience with *How Many?* conversations:

1. Have a student state their number but not their unit and then challenge the class to figure out what unit the student counted.

2. Reverse it. Have a student state their unit, but not how many they see. Challenge the class to figure out how many of that unit the student sees.

3. Make a list of *all* the different numbers—without units—that students see. Challenge the class to find at least one unit for each number.

4. Reverse the last one, too. Make a list of all the different units students see—without numbers. Challenge the class to find a correct count for each unit listed. I'll offer a word of caution on this last one: it works best with an image that has plenty of units with familiar natural-language names. For example, the pizza pages offer *slice, topping, pizza, cut,* and so on as units that students are likely to have words for. The page with an egg carton is not as rich with unit names.

Small Group

You may choose to have students work through some *How Many?* images in pairs or small groups—especially after the routines have been established through whole-class discussions. You could select about five prompts and have students move at their own pace through the set. If you allow enough time for everyone to get through three of the prompts, you'll likely give enough challenge to your faster-moving students while letting your slower-moving students have enough time to engage. Remember that this isn't about speed. Deep thinking about a small number of prompts is preferable to rushing through a bunch of them under time pressure. Noticing interesting details and relationships takes time.

Not everyone needs to do all of the same prompts. Depending on your classroom environment and traditions, you may want to have students record some product of their small-group work. They can record on paper, mini whiteboards, or tablets quite naturally. Typing responses on laptops or Chromebooks is likely to impede the kinds of work students will want to do, which often includes drawing diagrams and arrows pointing to parts of shapes.

One-on-One (or Two)

I have had a tremendous amount of fun with *How Many?* conversations in classrooms—anywhere from twenty-two kindergarteners to a doubled-up collection of fifty second graders to more than 100 parents and children at a family math night. But my absolute favorite context is sitting down with one reading partner or maybe two. At home, this is the standard; at school, it's a luxury. But if it turns out to be a luxury you can afford—ever—do it. Two math minds paying close, careful attention and delighting in each other's ideas—this is the best. Make time for it if you can.

Classroom Library

Put a couple of copies of *How Many?* in your classroom library. File it with the other nonfiction books and give students an opportunity to think quietly, to look deeply, and to create their own individual counting experiences.

Bulletin Board

A *How Many?* bulletin board might have several images and a collection of sticky notes and pens. Students can write their counts and their units on sticky notes and affix them next to the images. Over the course of several days, these notes can accumulate and become deeper and more complicated. Surely, one of your students will eventually think to put a sticky note on the board that reads "4 *How Many?* pictures" or "112 sticky notes!"

Parent Night

Parents know how to support their children's developing literacy from an early age. We have a clear, actionable message around reading—read for twenty minutes with your child every day. We lack a similarly simple message in mathematics. With reading, we know that the very act of reading together—whatever the parent and child read— supports developing literacy. The same is true in math. If parents and children talk about numbers, patterns, and shapes together, the children will be better prepared for later success in mathematics. *How Many?* conversations are a wonderful addition to a standard parent math night or open house. You don't need to do anything different than you would for a classroom full of children—just model the same behaviors and give parents and children an opportunity to play with counting ideas together. My experience is that parents who already integrate math talk in their daily lives find *How Many?* delightful right away and see the potential for new conversations beyond the confines of the book and that parents who don't already do much math talk at home find the open nature of the prompts liberating. Once this latter group understands that literally anything in the image can be the right thing to count, these parents often describe a feeling of freedom—freedom from the answer key and freedom from being wrong.

In short, I highly recommend adding a few pages' worth of whole-group *How Many?* conversations to your school's next parent event.

RESOURCES FOR GOING BEYOND THIS BOOK

Whatever format you use for your *How Many?* conversations, you'll eventually come to the end of the book. Fortunately, this doesn't mean you need to come to the end of the conversation. Here are several resources for finding and sharing additional prompts to keep you and your fellow learners thinking and talking about *How Many?*

1. My blog *Talking Math with Your Kids* (talkingmathwithyourkids.com). Type "How many?" into the search box there, and you will find articles recounting conversations I have had with my own children, together with the prompts that inspired them. You'll also find images I have found or created that supplement the book.

2. The website Number Talk Images (ntimages.weebly.com), maintained by Pierre Tranchmontagne, consists of a wonderful collection of beautiful images of mathematically structured objects in the world. From blueberries to arrays of heart stickers to dandelions and banana sculptures, you'll find great prompts for *How Many?* conversations here.

3. On Twitter, the hashtag #unitchat will turn up images and stories from teachers around the world. Find images to use there, share your own, and join the conversation!

Hopefully your *How Many?* conversations will begin to change how you see the world. Hopefully you'll start to notice ambiguous groupings, interesting arrangements, and new possibilities for counting things in your everyday world. When this begins to happen (if it has not already), I encourage you to practice capturing the things you notice and to share them on social media platforms. Next, I'll offer you a few quick tips for making high-quality images yourself.

DEVELOPING YOUR OWN *HOW MANY?* IMAGES

Time invested in selecting and framing images tends to pay off in the quality of conversations learners are able to have. If students are so focused on a person making a funny face in the background that no one notices the rich structures in the foreground, or if they spend too much time trying to figure out what in the world they're looking at, the ratio of quality mathematics to time spent can decrease rapidly. Here, then, are a few tips for selecting and making images with a higher likelihood of generating good *How Many?* conversations.

Look for Multiple Units

Throughout the book *How Many?,* the images have multiple units. It's not just that there are multiple things to count (e.g., pizzas and plates); it's that there are things you can count in multiple ways (e.g., whole pizzas and slices of pizza). If you make multiple units the focal point of your image, you'll have at least one extra layer of mathematical depth that will take a moment for students to notice and to talk about. There are lots of things that come in groups with names, and, similarly, there are lots of things in the world that get new names when you cut them into pieces. Look for examples in your life and in your students' lives.

Make It Clear

It's fun to have a variety of things to count, but having too many things distracts from the conversation. Keep background clutter to a minimum and help students focus on a smaller, related variety of counting targets.

Fill the Frame

When I first started capturing mathematical images for use with my students, I wasn't very bold. I would take a quick picture from whatever angle was convenient or easy—even in my own home. It's like I thought the marshmallows would be shy about having their photo taken, so I needed to do it quickly while they weren't paying attention. These images turned out not to work as well by the time I projected them in front of a crowded classroom. Now I understand that I need to take my time, get right up in the marshmallows' faces (figuratively speaking, of course), and fill the frame with the thing I want my students to see. This isn't *Where's Waldo?* where the fun is in hunting for a small thing hidden in a sea of noise. This is about drawing learners' attention to bold images of mathematical relationships in the world.

Attend to Lighting

Shadows can be trouble and can make it harder to distinguish the subject of your photograph. I have a favorite spot on my porch that gets lots of indirect natural light, and I can be spotted out there in all sorts of weather with odd arrangements of groceries. (My son, Griffin, recently declared, "Here's how you can tell Dad's working on a math book. He buys a bunch of sweet junk that he would normally think is gross and starts taking pictures.") Keep an eye out for similar spots in your own home and school—well-lighted, lightly trafficked areas where you can take a minute or two to compose your photo. Of course, there are lots of great *How Many?* images that are at too large a scale to let you choose your vantage point. Objects on the scale of trains, parking lots, buildings, large crowds of people, and trees may provide some great *How*

Many? conversations, but you can't pick where to photograph them. You can usually pick the angle, though, and sometimes even the time of day or the weather. In any case, developing a habit of considering the options for lighting before taking a picture will—over time—increase the quality of the math you and your students are able to discuss.

WHY WE DO THIS WORK

In this chapter, I have shared structures and principles that have served me and other teachers well in using *How Many?* to get children to think in original and creative ways about numbers and units. I think of this Teacher's Guide as a similar prompt for teachers. I trust that you will make these ideas your own and build new ideas from them. For me, the purpose of teaching is to help people make new things and see new relationships that will enrich their lives and the lives of others.

To that last point, my son, Griffin, was twelve years old and deep in an early adolescent phase of rejecting everything that those who love him held dear. In my case, this meant putting up with scorn for my love of mathematics. We were driving around on errands one evening, talking about upcoming events in the family, when I mentioned to him that I would be leading a parent math night at a local suburban school and so would not be around the house that evening. He proceeded to give me a hard time about my nerdiness. I responded from the heart.

"Griffin, let me tell you a little bit about my perspective on this whole Talking Math with Your Kids thing," I began, referring to my blog and associated projects. "My goal with this work has never been to have you and your sister fall in love with math. That would be great, but I can't control what you like or don't like. No, my goal has been to make sure that whatever you and your sister *do* want to do in life, the math required to do it doesn't get in the way or—even better—you can use math to do that thing well.

"You love to argue," I observed. "And there have been a number of times when I have noticed your arguments have had a math basis, or where a critique you have of how something is set up or labeled in the world depends on noticing that someone got the math wrong. So feel free to give me a hard time but also know that I can see the effects of this work in how you do the things you love to do. So from my perspective? Mission accomplished."

It was silent in the back seat for a few seconds before he replied.

"You should probably say that at the math night," he said.

So I did. And now I have said it to you. Let's do this together.

CHAPTER 4
Children Are Brilliant Mathematicians

One evening when my son, Griffin, was six years old, he was eager to have me do something with him (we have both since forgotten what that thing was). I was busy and told him I needed two more minutes to finish up. In order to hold me accountable, he proclaimed that he would count to 120 and that he would run laps of our house's first floor while doing so. Perhaps this was mainly a clever gambit for gaining my attention, and if it was, I bit hard by getting out my Flip camera (this was 2010) and filming him in action. You can watch the resulting video at https://vimeo.com/23501648. His younger sister, Tabitha—four years old at the time—wanted in on the action. She insisted I make a video of her counting, too (https://vimeo.com/23543507). The six-year-old ran and counted nearly flawlessly; the four-year-old made a number of predictable counting errors along the way as she counted (almost) to thirty.

For many children, counting is the introduction to mathematics. Sometimes adults see counting as a prerequisite for mathematical activity—a thing that is straightforward and unproblematic, and that children must master before they can do real math. In fact, counting is more complicated and interesting than this. Counting *is* real mathematics, and it is not complete when the child can correctly count collections of individual objects.

I used to think that the surface features of these videos told a fairly complete story of children's counting development. Griffin had mastered the counting sequence to 120 (and probably far beyond); Tabitha struggled in the teens, skipped twenty, and went straight to twenty-one, and so forth. As I have watched these children develop, and as I have studied children's learning more broadly, I now see much more going on in this scene. Now I see Griffin counting seconds while Tabitha is reciting number words. I notice that seconds are rather abstract units to count, and so they afford Griffin and me fewer opportunities to play with grouping and naming than if he were counting something more tangible such as eggs, shoes, or pizza slices.

This chapter aims to provide the reader with similar shifts in perspective. I hope to help you uncover complexity in what seems simple on the surface; to find wonder in things you thought you already knew. In service of this goal, I'll invite you into classrooms and conversations where children are doing rich mathematical thinking as they clarify the things they are counting, use the structures they notice, and uncover deep, important mathematical relationships.

WHAT CAN WE LEARN FROM SHOELACES?

While visiting a local school to talk about *How Many?* with students of a variety of ages, I found myself taking a straw poll of second graders. I had introduced the book to the

approximately fifty seven- and eight-year-olds assembled that morning by explaining that I was interested in what *they* saw in these images and that we would be diligent and precise in our conversations. They put me to the test almost immediately when the second child I called on said that she saw four laces in Figure 4.1.

"Four ends on the laces?" I asked.

"No. Four laces," she replied.

I paused to think.

"So each shoe has two laces?" I asked.

FIGURE 4.1
Does each shoe have one lace or two?

"Yup," she said with confidence.

In moments such as this, I have learned that when one child says something unexpected it often represents the unspoken thinking of many children. Hence, the straw poll.

"Second graders! I need to know what you think here. Does each shoe have two laces, so there are four laces in this picture? Or does each shoe have one lace, so there are two total laces in this picture?" We did a show of hands, and there was a clear majority—about two-to-one—in favor of two laces per shoe.

Do not discount these results until you have polled a group of young children yourself, as I have reproduced this experiment in a wide variety of kindergarten, first-, and second-grade classrooms. Almost every time, a majority of the children vote in favor of two laces per shoe, and almost every time their teachers take this in with the same look of surprise on their faces that I must have had the first time I watched all those second-grade hands go up.

Where does this idea come from, and why is it so pervasive? A premise of *How Many?* is that children's mathematical ideas—in particular, their ideas about numbers—are based first and foremost in the experiences of their lives. By the age of seven—when many students are in second grade—most children have learned to tie their shoes. As they learn and practice shoe tying, their experience is of having two things on each shoe. One crosses over the other, then tucks underneath, et cetera. Furthermore, children at this age are growing fairly quickly. Likely, they outgrow their shoes before they need to replace a shoelace. Children have experienced the twoness of shoelaces, and they have had no opportunity to encounter their oneness. So, of course, they tend to believe that each shoe has two laces.

An alternative hypothesis exists, though. Maybe this is a question of language. Maybe when I ask, "Does each shoe have two laces?" children hear, "Does each shoe have two *ends* to its shoelace?" I have two pieces of evidence to refute this hypothesis. The first is that children themselves tell me when I ask that they do not mean two *ends*; they mean two *laces*. The second piece of evidence is that several times I have unlaced my own shoe in front of a class of primary-grade children to great delight and surprise all around when it turns out to be just one. (I have also spotted more than a few unlaced shoes following a spirited *How Many?* session.)

When I have asked this same question of fifth graders, I have found myself on the wrong end of a classroom full of the kind of icy stares older children reserve for condescending adults asking trick questions. Fifth graders—as a group—are well aware that each shoe has a single lace. It must be that sometime between the ages of seven and eleven, most children either break a shoelace or want laces that are differently colored from the ones that came in a pair of shoes.

This story illustrates that counting—a seemingly simple practice that serves in part as a gateway to mathematical activity—is grounded in children's experiences. Those second graders I told you about were not taking wild guesses about the number of shoelaces in each shoe. Those fifth graders giving me icy stares had not experienced a unit of study on the Mathematics of Clothing with a standard about correctly enumerating the laces in shoes. In both cases the ideas grew from children's experiences, and these experiences inform children's mathematical thinking in many ways and at a variety of levels.

A PAIR OF EGGS

People sometimes describe math as "a universal language." This is only partly true. In one sense, 2 + 2 = 4 expresses an idea that is universally true. But our understanding of this truth is dependent on language. How do you *know* that 2 + 2 = 4? Most likely, you turn to an example in a context. *If I have two cookies, and you give me two more cookies, then I have four cookies.* Our ways of knowing depend on language that is not universal (here *cookie* is an English word, and a concept that not all cultures share), and our ability to communicate our mathematical ideas is similarly dependent on language. Furthermore, children learning mathematics behave a lot like children learning language, but this is not because math is a universal language. It is because mathematical ideas are tightly tied to the natural language in which we express them.

For example, a routine conversation I have with children when we discuss the shoes page is about two ways of counting the shoes. Some people look at the shoes and see *two*: two shoes. Other people look at the shoes and see *one*: one pair of shoes. I emphasize that these are two ways of viewing the same thing and that part of our work together will be to notice when that's possible. One day, this discussion with a class of

FIGURE 4.2
A pair of eggs, according to a first-grader

first graders led one boy to use the word "pair" in an interesting way.

We were on the page with a 3-by-4 array of eggs (see Figure 4.2) when this student announced that he saw "one pair of eggs."

I paused and thought for a moment, looking at the screen. I tried to identify which two eggs seemed to be paired together. I chose the two in the upper right for no good reason except to keep the conversation moving. "Do you mean this pair here?"

"No," he replied.

"This pair?" I asked, pointing to another two eggs somewhat haphazardly chosen.

"No," he said. "All of them are one."

While he had the wrong word, the idea was exactly right. *All of them are one.* Children do not need to have precise language in order for their ideas to be valid, mathematically important contributions to a community's understanding. The imprecise language of *pair* allowed this child to express an idea that he generalized from our discussion—you can take all of the things, put them in a group, use a new word to refer to that group, and count the group as one.

The band They Might Be Giants has a terrific song titled "There's Only One Everything." The song's title is itself an invitation to play with units: What is there one of? But the lyrics are delightful, also. One verse invites children to imagine drawing a giant circle around everything there is. "Would there still be something left on the outside? And does that question even make any sense?" The band invites young children to play with the idea of units; it suggests the possibility of playful thinking about place value and groups.

FIGURE 4.3
One way of showing how many tens are in thirty-two

$$
\begin{array}{r}
10 \\
\times\ 3 \\
\hline
30
\end{array}
$$

While They Might Be Giants and *How Many?* make units and groups into literal child's play, these ideas are quite challenging. When I have asked the future elementary teachers in my math courses *How many tens are in 268?* the majority of my students have tended to say *six*. Persuading them that this is the correct answer to a different question, but a wrong answer to this one, takes several weeks' worth of challenging place value-study.

I once asked my daughter, Tabitha, how many tens are in 268. She was seven years old at the time and said there are 26 tens in 268. I followed up by asking, "What would you say to someone who said there are six tens in 268?"

She replied, "I'd say there are a lot more than that."

This pretty much sums up the matter. *How many tens in 268?* is like *How many nines in 268?* The second question is unambiguous. It asks us to find the number of groups of nine in 268, and so we divide. There are twenty-nine of those groups and some leftovers. The beautiful thing about tens is that they are built right into our number system. How do you *know* there are twenty-nine nines in 268? There's some work to do. How do you *know* there are twenty-six tens in 268? If you have a rich understanding of place value, the work is considerably less. It's written right there!

As part of my effort to persuade my students and future teachers that six is not the ideal answer to this question, we watch a video (from Philipp, Cabral, and Schappelle, 2005) of a girl answering similar questions.

"How many tens are in thirty-two?" an interviewer asks.

"Three," the girl replies.

"And how do you know that there are three tens?" the interviewer asks. The girl proceeds to write the multiplication on paper as in Figure 4.3.

"Ten times three is thirty," she says as she writes.

My students and I ask two questions of ourselves: (1) Does this child understand place value? and (2) What question would you want to ask her in order to better assess her knowledge? In the end, we want to know whether she understands that "How many tens are in 32?" is a special question. It is like "How many nines are in 32?" but also unique due to the structure of our number system. We want to know whether she understands both of these things—the similarity to *how many nines* and the uniqueness of *how many tens.*

The typical American elementary math curriculum presumes that understanding place value precedes studying multiplication and division. In fact, rich understanding of place value requires that these ideas be intertwined. In Chapter 2, I wrote about the meaning of multiplication, and I argued that for most students the foundational meaning of multiplication involves groups. A x B means A groups of B. The girl in the video sees thirty-two as three groups of ten, plus two. For her, the ideas of multiplication and of place value are developing in tandem rather than one after the other.

This observation has implications for classroom teaching—we should expect that learning place value well is a long-term project rather than a thing that happens in a small number of weeks. More specifically, the observation that children use their developing multiplication knowledge to learn place value well is a reason that I included lots of opportunities to notice, discuss, and count groups in *How Many?* A pair of shoes, a dozen eggs, a row of avocado halves, a bowl of grapefruit . . . each of these groups is like ten. Each offers the opportunity to work on both multiplicative thinking and foundational ideas about place value.

Another conversation with my daughter (who was seven years old at the time) took place in a thoughtful moment one summer evening as we looked out the window at the top of the stairs to the second floor of our home, watching storm clouds roll in. I asked her, "How many tens are in thirty-two?" She said three. I asked her how she knew and she counted ten, twenty, thirty on her fingers.

A moment passed and she said, "There are ten tens in a hundred, though."

"But how many in 200?" I asked.

"Twenty," she said.

"Whoa," I said, and she said, "Yeah."

Another silent moment passed, and she offered this simple observation: "Asking 'How many tens are in thirty?' is like asking 'How many ones are in two?'"

A major challenge in elementary math teaching is that many deeply complex ideas are captured in seemingly simple terms. Of course, this is also a beautiful thing about teaching elementary math. Tabitha's observation about asking *How many tens are in 30?* is an example of both the beauty of elementary math and the tension between simplicity and complexity that is present there.

Viewed through the lens of simplicity, Tabitha's claim boils down to *There are three tens in thirty,* which is both simple and true. But there is more to her claim, and this is where the complexity arises. Tabitha's claim is not just about how many tens in thirty, it is also about how two questions are related: *How many tens are in thirty?* is like *How many ones are in two?*

Tabitha saw thirty as being like two and ten as being like one. In what ways are these objects alike, and are the similarities based on these particular numbers or are the structures more general? The moment has passed, so I cannot go back and ask seven-year-old Tabitha this question, but a reasonable interpretation based on what I know about her place value knowledge over time, and on what I know about children's place value thinking more generally, is that she intended to point to thirty and two as examples of whole classes of numbers, but to ten and one as special cases. She could just as easily have claimed that "Asking how many tens are in forty is the same as asking how many ones are in five." But she would likely have rejected a counterclaim that "Asking how many sixes are in thirty is like asking how many ones are in two."

In that moment, she was likely expressing that one and ten are special and that the decades (ten, twenty, thirty, etc.) have the same relationship with ten that one-digit numbers have with one—namely, that questions about how many are answered directly by the numbers themselves. Thirty means three tens. Whether this insight was based on Tabitha's knowledge of number language, numeration, or (more likely) a combination of these of which she may not even have been aware, we won't ever know. But we can say with confidence that she understood that ten is special.

An important question remains unanswered in this story. We don't know whether she thought asking *How many hundreds in 300?* was like these other two questions. That is to say, we don't know whether she could—in that moment—generalize how ones, tens, hundreds, thousands, and so on are the building blocks of place value. I definitely know from later conversations with her that she had not yet mastered the corresponding generalization about fractional place value: *Asking how many ones are in two is like asking how many tenths are in 0.3.* (This final point recalls the question from Chapter 2 about how to read 0.5 aloud.)

Tabitha's observation is a more nuanced application of unitizing than "All of them are one," and it comes from having multiple experiences making, breaking, counting, and discussing groups. In particular, her observation builds an essential bridge from *groups are important* to *groups of ten are special*. This is the essential question my students were left with when watching the *How many tens in thirty-two?* video earlier, and it is worth comparing the evidence we have that the girl in the video understands the special nature of ten against the evidence that Tabitha did on that stormy summer evening. Recall that the girl in the video justified the number of tens in thirty-two the same way that one might justify the number of sixes in thirty-two—by reference to the corresponding multiplication fact. While this doesn't rule out place-value understanding, it also doesn't provide evidence in favor of it. Tabitha's comparison, by contrast, explicitly named ten as a unit: ten, like one, is a thing you can count.

The progression in this section has been one of increasing sophistication. At the outset, a boy seemed to be quite early in the stages of thinking and talking about groups. When he used *pair* to refer to a group of a dozen eggs, he seemed to be experimenting with the ways natural language can express the mathematical idea of grouping. At the end of this section, we heard Tabitha making a claim about the specialness of a particular size of group—ten. Having mastered some beginning ideas about number language and grouping, we heard her playing with connections and making insights as she did so.

MATH REQUIRES DEFINITIONS

"I see twelve eggshells," a first-grade girl told me while her class considered a photograph of a dozen eggs (see Figure 4.4). I immediately had a follow-up question.

"What if I cracked open one of those eggs to make a fried egg?" I asked, miming the cracking and opening of a single egg into a pan, each hand retaining an imaginary half of the original eggshell. "How many eggshells would there be then?"

"Well, you made that one into two. So I think it's thirteen." She replied thoughtfully.

"So if I break open an egg, one eggshell becomes two?" I asked.

"Yes," she said with a knowing smile. "And if you broke those, you'd have more."

"Class!" I cried. "Let's stop and think about this for a moment. The claim is that when you break an eggshell, you get two eggshells, not two *half*-eggshells. Can you think of any other things that work like that?"

This is a complicated idea at the boundary of language and math. The class needed a little help thinking it through, which I provided.

"If you cut a sandwich in half, you don't have two sandwiches, right? And if you break a pencil, you don't have two pencils. But eggshells are different. Breaking an eggshell gives us two (or more) eggshells. I wonder if eggshells are the only things that work like that."

Together we considered many possibilities, including pizzas (no—you get *slices* of pizza by cutting, not *pizzas*), slices of pizza (controversial—some children had experience with half-slices of pizza), and squares (no, but yes if you cut them in fourths in just the right

FIGURE 4.4
Twelve eggshells

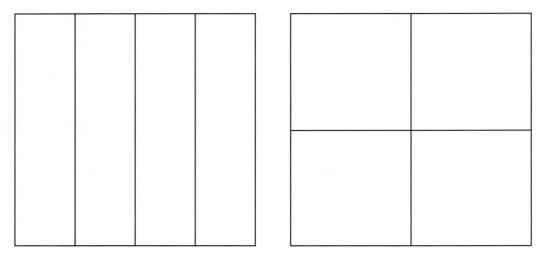

FIGURE 4.5
When you cut squares into fourths, you sometimes get squares and sometimes not.

way as in Figure 4.5). Like many conversations prompted by the ambiguous question *How many?* the point of this one was not to come to consensus, nor to reveal a correct answer. In creatively imagining the nature of a variety of familiar units, these children were engaged in rich mathematical thinking. This conversation was about clarity of thought and precision of language. *What do these words that we use all the time really mean? Who gets to decide what they mean? Does anybody actually decide this, or is it something we all have to figure out for ourselves?*

At a more advanced level, former students of a colleague of mine—Minneapolis middle school teacher Annie Perkins—spontaneously wrote her a note after their first week of high school. All teachers enjoy hearing from former students, but Annie was especially delighted by the form and content of their note. They wrote to inform her that the work they had done in her class around precision and definitions had begun to infect their ways of viewing the world. In particular, they had determined that one pretzel becomes two pretzels when it is broken in half. They found this result surprising, but completely undeniable in light of the definition of pretzel that they found on Wikipedia. That definition referred to pretzels as being a bread-based product commonly shaped like a knot. Because the shape is not a required part of the definition, and because the pretzel pieces are still bread-based, there is nothing to exclude each piece from being a pretzel. In Figure 4.6, each of the two parts of the original pretzel satisfies the Wikipedia definition by being a bread-based product and having all characteristics other than shape in common with the original. Therefore, each is a pretzel.

The conversation about eggshells relied on everyday usage and familiarity with eggshells. In first grade, we drew our conclusions based on our experiences with eggshells, pizzas, and slices. In high school, students can draw conclusions based on established definitions. The latter is more sophisticated and abstract, but it is a version of exactly the same activity. In both cases, learners are thinking about the meanings of words and about the consequences of these meanings.

Indeed, there is lots of fun and interesting work to be done with definitions before children get to first grade. A friend's daughter, Maria, announced at the age of three that "a sandwich has three things," which turned out to be two slices of bread and a filling. Her mother—teacher Megan Schmidt—shared this with me on Twitter (knowing a thing or two about my interest in children's minds), which led to Megan mediating a conversation between me and Maria in which I probed Maria's claims, seeking to find the limits of her definition. Eventually, we arrived at the question of whether an Oreo cookie is a sandwich.

FIGURE 4.6
Does breaking a pretzel yield two pretzels?

Her mother asked on my behalf as she handed the child an Oreo. "Maria, I have a question. Is this a sandwich?"

Maria examined it carefully and said, "Um, no. It's not."

"Why isn't this a sandwich?" her mother asked

"It doesn't have things, like a burger," Maria replied.

This was an important moment. Maria needed a word to describe the thing she saw as missing from an Oreo, and she adapted a word to describe it. The filling of a sandwich is the *burger*.

Her mother stacked two Oreos and asked, "Is this a sandwich?"

Maria examined this new construction even more closely. "No. It doesn't have stuff in it. It needs lots of stuff inside like a burger to be a sandwich. I want a burger. Let's get one," she suggested, and with a face full of Oreos, she declared, "We won't tell Daddy."

About a week later, Maria's mother passed along an update. Maria had reported that marshmallows between two graham crackers counted as a sandwich because "there's a burger," but that Oreos still did not count as sandwiches. In the interim, Maria's mother

had opened an Oreo to ensure that Maria was aware of the filling, and Maria had rejected the Oreo as a sandwich on new grounds—the burger is white.

This three-year-old had an extraordinarily precise definition. A sandwich is made of three things—two slices of bread and a non-white burger. It seemed to me that the graham crackers and marshmallow were an exception to the white burger rule. I asked about that and learned that their marshmallows were pink! (See Figure 4.7.)

FIGURE 4.7
This is a sandwich because the burger isn't white.

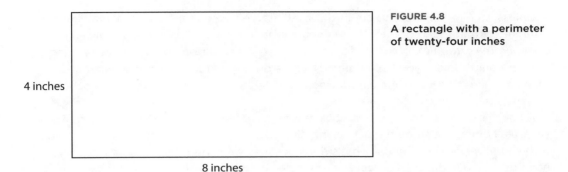

FIGURE 4.8
A rectangle with a perimeter of twenty-four inches

4 inches

8 inches

While the intellectual work children do when defining eggshells or pretzels or sandwiches is clear, it may not be obvious to the world that this intellectual activity is mathematical. I'll make that argument next, by way of examples.

The rectangle in Figure 4.8 has a perimeter of twenty-four inches and whole-number side lengths. Take a moment to sketch a different rectangle that also has a perimeter of twenty-four units with whole-number side lengths.

Is your rectangle the only solution? How many solutions are there? That is, how many different rectangles have whole-number side lengths and a perimeter of twenty-four units? There are four common answers to the question *How many?* depending on the definitions of *rectangle* and *different* that you have in mind. For example, if you think of a rectangle as having two short sides and two long sides, then you're likely to say that there are either ten or five different rectangles—ten different rectangles if you're counting the 1-by-11 rectangle as different from the 11-by-1 rectangle or five if you count them as the same. Those are two of the most common answers.

But the "two short sides and two long sides" definition of a rectangle doesn't allow for a square. If you define a rectangle as a parallelogram with a right angle (or some other equivalent definition that doesn't depend on having two different side lengths), then a square counts as a rectangle, and you'll have either eleven or six different rectangles with whole-number side lengths and a perimeter of twenty-four units. These are the other two most common answers.

Unless, that is, you want to count a 0-by-12 figure as a rectangle (mathematicians often refer to this kind of thing as *the degenerate case,* so a 0-by-12 rectangle is a *degenerate rectangle*). In that case, you need to add either one or two more rectangles to your count. Unless you have defined "whole numbers" to mean numbers greater than zero, in which case zero isn't a whole number, so you don't need to count the degenerate rectangle.

All of this is to say that mathematics relies on precise definitions in order to make sure we are all doing the same thing. Lacking careful definitions of *rectangle, different,* and *whole number,* we can't know what's right because we cannot know what's true. We need precision in order to agree on our results. In this case, an important result is that of all rectangles with the same perimeter, the square always has the largest area. Useful mathematical results that are known to be true are called *theorems.* This particular theorem depends on counting squares as rectangles.

A second example of the importance of precise definitions in mathematical work comes from geometry. Where the first example involved measurement, this one involves relationships among geometric objects.

A square has four sides and four vertices. Do all shapes have the same number of sides as vertices? Before reading the following discussion, take a moment to determine the number of sides and vertices in each of the shapes in Figure 4.9.

Let's consider these shapes from left to right. The triangle has three sides and three vertices. The line segment has two endpoints. Whether these are vertices depends on

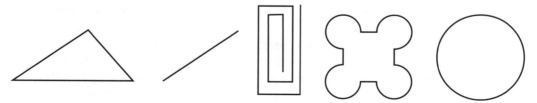

FIGURE 4.9
Do all shapes have the same number of sides as vertices?

whether you count an endpoint as a vertex. A common, entry-level definition of *vertex* is "where two sides come together." The endpoints on the line segment do not connect sides, so by this definition, the line segment has one side and zero vertices. If, however, you do count the endpoints as vertices (perhaps by defining a vertex as the end of a side), then the line segment has one side and two vertices. Either way, the number of sides is not equal to the number of vertices. The rectangular paper clip has endpoints, as the line segment does, but it would be difficult to say that it has no vertices at all. It has nine sides and either eight or ten vertices, depending on whether you count endpoints as vertices. The castle-shaped figure has eight places where edges seem to come together, but if you define a vertex to be the place where two *straight* sides come together then it has none. There is no mathematical need to define vertices this way. Notice that I have implicitly referred to the circles at each corner of the castle as sides, and again this is a matter of definition. If a line must be straight to be a side, then the castle has only four sides. But then we would need a word for the curvy things we're no longer calling sides.

This brings us to the last shape in the collection—the circle. A circle is commonly said to have zero sides, but if the castle has eight sides, the circle must have one. Finally, mathematicians often think of a circle as the end of a process. Start with an equilateral triangle, with side lengths of four inches (so twelve inches altogether). Now imagine this triangle is made of a stiff string-like material that is easy to straighten or to bend at any angle. Transform the triangle into a square with three-inch side lengths. Then make it into a regular pentagon, then a hexagon, a heptagon, an octagon, and so on (see Figure 4.10). After you've done this a couple dozen times, the sides will be so short that it will be difficult to distinguish your polygon from a circle. Now imagine that this process goes on forever. At the end of that process you would have a polygon with infinitely many sides, each infinitely short; you would have a circle. This kind of thinking is at the heart of calculus. While the objects under consideration here—sides, vertices, polygons, and circles—are more obviously mathematical than sandwiches, the *process* is the same. In both cases, we are using definitions to decide what's true, and in both cases, we are using new objects (such as Oreos and castles) to give our definitions a test drive.

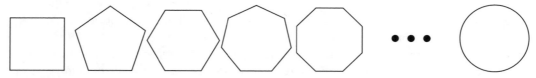

FIGURE 4.10
A circle can be seen as a polygon with infinitely many sides.

This activity is deeply mathematical regardless of the nature of the objects—whether they come from the physical world or an abstract, mathematical one. Therefore, having extended conversations in which students carefully specify what they are counting is time well spent in teaching mathematics. "When will I ever have to use this?" the student asks while studying the quadratic formula, the long-division algorithm, or triangle circumcenters. A common response in schools is to claim that studying these things teaches students to think. If we are to make good on that promise to students— that studying school mathematics will enable them to apply their minds to solving the real problems their future selves will encounter—then we need to deploy the tools of mathematicians frequently and sincerely. We need to take seriously students' claims about objects and their definitions, and we need to develop an expectation that definitions have consequences. *How Many?* provides a rich territory for exactly this kind of mathematical activity; I encourage you and your students to spend the time necessary to explore it thoroughly. In my experience, asking about eggshells is a reliable way to invite learners of all ages to discuss definitions in a low-stakes way that supports participation by a wide range of students.

AVOCADOS AND WHAT THEY CAN TELL US ABOUT NUMBER PROPERTIES

Definitions formalize the meanings of words; there is also math in the grammar with which these words are assembled. A careful *How Many?* conversation can draw out this grammar and its associated mathematics. The following story is an example of this using half-avocados.

FIGURE 4.11
The associative property of multiplication lurks in the avocado array.

When visiting a college algebra classroom at a local high school, I used the avocados page (see Figure 4.11) as an icebreaker—a way to help the students get to know me before launching into the abstract work of rates, graphs, and functions. Avocados may be less abstract, but they are no less rigorous. After a moment to think, and another to converse with a partner, the class readily agreed that there were fifteen half-avocados in the picture.

"Did anyone see seven and one-half in this picture?" I asked the class.

One young man raised his hand.

"Nice. Thank you. What did you see seven and one-half of?" I asked.

"Avocados," he replied warily.

"How do you know there are seven and one-half avocados?" I asked.

"Because fifteen divided by two is seven and one-half," he said.

"OK. Good. Do we agree with this, class?" I asked, and they indicated they did.

"Right. So some of us counted fifteen half-avocados, and others of us counted fifteen divided by two avocados," I said, as I wrote the following on the board:

15 (half-avocados)

($\frac{15}{2}$) avocados

"And we know," I continued, "that fifteen divided by two is the same as fifteen halves." I replaced *($\frac{15}{2}$) avocados* with *(15 halves) avocados* so that the board now looked like this:

15 (half-avocados)

(15 halves) avocados

"How many half-avocados? Fifteen. How many avocados? Fifteen halves. Apart from treating *half* as singular or plural, the only difference between these two phrases is the grouping," I asserted. We discussed whether this was only the case for avocados, or only true of halves, or of the number fifteen, and we agreed that the principle was true no matter what units, fractions, or numbers we were working with.

Indeed, this is true. Twenty-seven (thirds of an apple) is equivalent to (twenty-seven thirds) apples. What is more, if we are multiplying three numbers—say, 2, 5, and 12—2 x (5 x 12) gives the same result as (2 x 5) x 12. Or more generally, a x (b x c) = (a x b) x c is a way of representing the *associative property of multiplication*. In an algebra course, an abstract statement of this property may seem to come out of the clear blue sky. But viewed as a way of formalizing things we already know but maybe don't attend to—in this case how numbers interact with units—it becomes a statement of familiar truth. Mathematics helps us express a relationship we already know to be true.

Mathematicians refer to multiplication as an *associative* operation because a x (b x c) = (a x b) x c. Division is not associative because (1 ÷ 2) ÷ 3 is not the same as 1 ÷ (2 ÷ 3). The first expression is equal to $\frac{1}{6}$; the second is equal to $\frac{3}{2}$. The associative property is about how you group things when you are multiplying several things. The *commutative property* of multiplication is about how you order them. 3 x 2 is the same as 2 x 3, and more generally a x b = b x a for all possible values of a and b. This is not true for division (try it!), so mathematicians say that multiplication is commutative while division is not. Noticing that the associative property applies even to units such as avocados leads naturally to wondering whether the commutative property applies, also. At least in English, you absolutely can make sensible, true, and numerically equivalent statements out of all possible rearrangements of *fifteen*, *half*, and *avocados*.

Perhaps you run a produce stand and someone has asked you how many avocados you have (as opposed to the peaches and grapefruit on display). You can reply "Avocados? Fifteen halves!"

Or maybe you and your partner are making guacamole. You are slicing and pulling out the pits while she prepares to mash them in a mortar and pestle. "Avocado halves!" you exclaim to inform her of your progress. "Fifteen!"

The English language's grammar of units and quantities is consistent with some important properties of multiplication. This isn't a trivial observation, because not all words work this way. Consider the case of the baker's half-dozen.

When we discuss *a dozen* as a unit, another unit often comes into play—*a baker's dozen*. While a dozen is a group of twelve, a baker's dozen is a dozen with one extra—an insurance policy on the part of bakers to avoid being accused of cheating the customer by shrinking the size of the individual baked goods. Standing in a checkout line at a large grocery store recently, I noticed that the woman in front of us was buying boxes of donuts, each labeled as containing "a baker's half-dozen" (see Figure 4.12). Before you read on, take a moment to guess how many donuts were in each box and to consider alternative possibilities to your first idea.

It turns out that a baker's half-dozen and half a baker's dozen are not the same thing. A baker's half-dozen (at least at this grocery store) contains half a dozen plus one more, for a total of seven donuts (see Figure 4.13). Half a baker's dozen should have

half of thirteen, or six and a half donuts. Elementary school children are capable of producing both seven and six and a half as possibilities for the number of donuts in a baker's half-dozen, and older students can extend the ideas to play with the (fictional) concept of a baker's gross. If a gross is a dozen dozens (144), how many should be in a baker's gross? As with the baker's half-dozen, can you think of more than one possibility?

Comparing a baker's half-dozen to half a baker's dozen seems like a language

FIGURE 4.12
How many donuts in a baker's half-dozen?

FIGURE 4.13
A baker's half-dozen is not the same as half a baker's dozen.

game on the surface. Beneath that surface are important mathematical ideas that include the associative and commutative properties and the order of operations. This is not to say that children need to learn the associative and commutative properties as prerequisites to learning their native tongue. Instead, it serves to remind us that mathematics grows out of people's experiences. Math is a way of formalizing these experiences and intuitive ideas and of exploring their consequences by asking new questions and probing at the corners of the intellectual space they create.

"Math is everywhere," yes. But not because you can apply math to every corner of your daily life. Math is everywhere because it is rooted there. Math grows from our rich experiences with language and pattern and play. Without experiences with sharing, there is no division. Without putting objects into groups, there is no multiplication, no place value. Without objects, there is no counting. This is how mathematics developed historically, and it is how math develops for children. *How Many?* provides one way of nurturing this growth in children by focusing their attention on important aspects of their everyday world that lead to productive mathematical work.

RELATIONSHIPS AND CONNECTIONS

Relationships and connections have an important role in learning. That children's minds are *blank slates* may be a common assumption in society, but it is certainly not true. We all try to make connections—to things we know, to things we believe or have experienced, and between seemingly disparate ideas. The first grader I told you about earlier, who said he saw one pair of eggs, was making a connection between shoes and eggs—they both come in groups. "All of them are one."

How Many? is designed to support students in making connections. While the language connection this first grader made isn't one I anticipated, I did design the sets so that *groups* would be a connection students would make. A pair of shoes, a dozen eggs, a bowl of grapefruit—these are all examples of groups that students are likely to notice, and they will be *more* likely to notice groups as they seek connections within and among the various sets of photos. On the pizza page, two slices on one plate make a serving, which is itself a group.

The opposite of grouping is partitioning. Partitioning involves cutting a thing into smaller pieces and naming these pieces—perhaps as their own units, perhaps using fraction notation or language. The relationship between grouping and partitioning is an example of an essential relationship in mathematics—they are *inverses*.

Two processes are inverses if each one undoes the other. Think of a number, any number. Add five to it. Now subtract five from that. You're back at the number you started with, and it doesn't matter what number you thought of at the beginning. Subtracting five always undoes adding five. It works the other way, too. If you start by subtracting five, and *then* add five, you'll end up with the number you started with. This is what mathematicians mean when they call addition and subtraction *inverse operations*. In the same way, multiplication and division are inverse operations (so long as you don't involve zero), as are squaring and finding the square root (so long as the numbers you start with are not negative).

It's the same for grouping and partitioning. "Two halves make a whole" means that you partition the whole into two equal pieces (*halves*) and then make a group of two of those to get back to where you started. Inverses are an idea that runs throughout mathematics. The two major topics of study in calculus—differentiation and integration—are inverses, for example.

And yet, this relationship is really only true in the abstract. Humpty Dumpty couldn't be put back together after his unfortunate experience of being partitioned, and there are plenty of everyday things (loaves of bread, raw eggs, vases) that children know can never be fully restored to their initial states after partitioning. "Two halves make a whole" requires us to ignore certain features of the real world—for example, crumbs—while we pay full attention to another—the total quantity. In order for this to seem natural—this abstract removal from certain details of our everyday experience—children need practice thinking about and noticing it. The real world can only support children's building of mathematical abstractions if they have opportunities to test the boundaries of the relationship between the two.

Mathematics is about relationships, not discrete disconnected facts. Yet the instructional routines and resources available to teachers often play down the relationships in favor of chopping big important ideas into individually digestible parts that children can't choke on. When these bite-sized morsels become the focus of attention, the original big ideas and their relationships get lost.

When I was in fourth grade, a major goal of my teacher was for me and my classmates to memorize our multiplication facts to 12. To this end, our classroom had a clothesline with twelve landmarks numbered 1 to 12. Each student's name was written on a clothespin and placed on the clothesline, starting at 1. Each Friday, we took a multiplication quiz in which we had one minute to recall each of the multiplication facts corresponding to the current location of our clothespin. In my mind's eye, I can still see the mimeographed half-sheets of paper on which these quizzes were printed. A key thing to know about these quizzes is that the facts were randomly scrambled. So if I was working on the "4" facts, the first line might be 4 x 11, the next might be 4 x 7, and so on. I would have to recall twelve facts—each beginning with 4, but each fact giving no clue about what the next one would be. As the school year progressed, my own clothespin trailed along, easily in the last 20 percent of the class, because I saw no value in facts without relationships. If we had been given two minutes, I could have thought about the facts in isolation. If the facts had been in order, I could have used the relationships to complete the quiz in under a minute. But speed was valued over relationships, and my clothespin moved slowly.

My son has a tremendous memory, so remembering multiplication facts was not a concern for him. His brain naturally stores disconnected bits of information that he can recall at will even after long periods of time have elapsed. My daughter is more like me, needing to use meaningful relationships to recall information. Both of them have used technology in their math classes, and nearly all of this technology has been in the same service as those mimeographed Friday quizzes of my youth. One piece of software my daughter has encountered is XtraMath, in which disconnected facts appear together with a ticking timer. She is immediately told whether her responses are right or wrong and—when wrong—she is *shown the digits that she ought to have typed!*

If teaching multiplication were anything like house-training puppies, then XtraMath would be a fine tool for the job. But teaching multiplication isn't anything like that at all. Multiplication is connected to other things, such as addition, division, place value, fractions, area, and algebra. We need to question whether providing the digits of the correct answer in outline form is appropriate support for building a robust concept of multiplication in which these ideas are connected and each helps to bring meaning to the others. Providing digits to trace in response to wrong answers suggests that when a student says that 6 x 5 is 43, the problem is that he has written down the wrong number—a problem that the software seeks to solve by forcing the student to write down the correct number. But if a student says that 6 x 5 is 43, it is much more likely that he does not understand something important about multiplication (for instance, that the product is equal to the total number of objects in six groups of five objects each). The software may train the student to write the correct digits in response to 6 x 5, but it won't have taught the student anything at all about multiplication or the ideas to which multiplication is connected.

There are strong forces in school mathematics that work against students seeing and using relationships. Training students to know things in isolation is detrimental to their engagement with real mathematical thinking and to their understanding of the nature of the discipline.

Unlike XtraMath or scrambled, mimeographed multiplication quizzes, *How Many?* is designed to support building relationships. The first set of images uses the relationship between a full box and an empty box to suggest zero. If you counted shoes or shoelaces or eyelets on the first page, you are likely to notice that there are zero of those things on the second page. Without that relationship, you would be more likely to count only the things that *are* in the image, not to count the things that aren't there. Later on, students use the fact that there were twelve eggs in the carton on one page to know that there are eight uncracked eggs on the next. They don't have to figure out all over again that the carton holds twelve.

On the first pizza page, students notice that there are six pizzas and that there is a pizza cutter in the image. They are likely to wonder how many slices each pizza will yield and then to speculate about the total there will be once the pizzas are sliced. If students guess that each pizza will give eight slices, they consider 6 x 8 in a meaningful, connected way, and they have all the time they need to think about how many slices that is. Maybe they see 6 x 8 as 3 x 8, doubled, or as 2 x 8 three times. The image supports both of these ways of thinking and more. For example, some students may use their 6 x 8 solution to figure out how many slices there actually are when they see that each pizza has six slices instead of the eight they anticipated. If you expected forty-eight slices,

then the fact that each pizza has two fewer slices means there must be twelve fewer slices altogether, or thirty-six slices in the six pizzas. The images on each page of *How Many?* support students in looking for relationships between the numbers they're thinking about, and the development of the images from one page to the next supports them in building relationships between prior results and new problems under consideration.

FIGURE 4.14
How many posts are required to separate twelve eggs? Does their arrangement matter?

FIGURE 4.15
How many posts are required to separate thirty eggs?

In a rich set of images, children will see things the author didn't intend. Frequently, children count the posts that separate the eggs in the 3-by-4 egg carton (see Figure 4.14). There are six of these posts. When someone mentions that, I tend to take the opportunity to ask whether the relationship between posts and eggs is always the same. "How many posts were in the 2-by-6 egg carton we saw on the previous page?" I'll ask. "Can you picture that in your head?" After discussing and resolving this question, I'll ask about the source of this difference. "Why do we sometimes need six posts to separate twelve eggs, and sometimes five posts? How many posts do we need to separate thirty eggs?" (see Figure 4.15).

How Many? is a book rich in relationships. I encourage you to look for and linger over these relationships with your students. Use this book to help them develop their understanding of mathematics as a discipline that depends on relationships. Use it also to help them develop a vision for mathematics—for seeing mathematical relationships in their everyday worlds, whether in the shoe store, in the grocery store, in their kitchens, or at their dining room tables. Math grows out of the relationships that surround us.

HOW MANY? AND *HOW MUCH?* IN TWELVE PARAGRAPHS OR LESS

"What's the difference between 'How many?' and 'How much'?" I asked a fifth grader recently.

"'How much' is using measurements. 'How many' is using numbers. Counting numbers," she replied.

That is about as cogent an explanation as a person of any age is likely to produce. "How many?" is a reasonable question to ask about grapefruit (or grapefruit halves). "How much?" is the right question to ask about grapefruit *juice*. Unless you're measuring the juice in countable units, in which case you may ask, "How many cups?"

Making things more precise, "How many?" is about units that have already been specified. "How much?" is about unsegmented wholes. Some "How much?" questions include:

- How much fruit should we buy at the grocery store?

- How much juice would you like for breakfast?

- How much wildlife did you see on vacation?

- How much clothing do we need to stay warm on a cold winter's day?

Once the units are specified, we can count these units and *How Much?* becomes *How Many?*

- How many apples should we buy?

- How many ounces of juice would you like?

- How many different kinds of birds did you see?

- How many layers should I wear under my jacket to stay warm today?

This fifth grader wasn't reciting a rule she had learned in school about when to use "how much?" and when to use "how many?" Instead, she was making explicit—perhaps

FIGURE 4.16
How much juice? How many cups of juice?

for the first time—a convention she had inferred from her experience with everyday language. It's a question that can easily arise when considering the grapefruit juice page (Figure 4.16).

After a series of discussions about How many rinds? How many glasses? and How many cabinets? someone might ask "What about *How many juice?*" This will sound funny, and then the class will be off and running. An added advantage of this kind of discussion is that it provides a bit of explicit language instruction for those with less experience with formal academic English.

For example, should the grocery express checkout lane say "12 items or less" or "12 items or fewer"? (And is it OK to buy two dozen eggs in that lane? What about two dozen apples? Does it matter whether the apples are bagged?) Sticklers for English grammar tend to insist on using "fewer" for things you can count and "less" for unsegmented wholes. Fewer grapefruits make less juice. Strangely, "more" applies to both.

Things get tricky when we try to apply English words to formal mathematical ideas, as when comparing numbers. Ten is bigger than five. Is ten bigger than −200? In math, we tend to use "greater than" and "less than" in order to eliminate this ambiguity. Formally, a number that lies to the right of another on the number line is the greater of the two. Whether you think of −200 as a "big" number, it is less than 5, which is less than 10. (And if you are disturbed by your local grocery store's "12 items or less" sign—just think of it as shorthand for "the number of items must be 12 or less than 12.")

In case you worry that *greater than* and *less than* are just examples of mathematicians making up rules for using words in order to make things more complicated, know that these distinctions are essential to mathematical practice. In calculus, for example, the lowercase Greek letter epsilon (ε) usually represents a very small positive number (such as 0.00000001), while N is frequently used to represent a large negative number (such as −1,000,000,000,000). *Small* and *large* here refer to each number's distance from zero, and if the meaning is likely to be at all unclear, there is formal language and symbolism to make the meaning specific.

All of this is to say that ideas are paramount, and words can develop as needed to express them. Comparing quantities and values is important work for elementary students, and the vocabulary for comparing can be formalized along with the ideas. Is anyone really confused by what the "12 items or less" sign is trying to tell us? Probably not, so maybe it doesn't actually matter. But if I ask students for the "smallest solution" to a problem, some may think I mean the solution that is closest to zero while others may think I mean the least solution. If −200 and 5 are both possible solutions, then the criteria for which solution is better are unclear. I need to be more precise. It's the same for student talk. Rather than correcting student language on the spot, use imprecise words as an opportunity to draw attention to the sometimes strange structures of language. Make comparisons in reading *How Many?* with your students. Listen to their language, and learn to hear the ideas that children mean their words to express. Identify and iron out ambiguity together in order to end up with clear and unambiguous claims.

COUNTING IS REAL MATHEMATICS

I have one final story about counting as an important and rich mathematical activity. At the beginning of this chapter, I told you about my son, Griffin, at six years old, who counted 120 seconds in order to hold me accountable to my promise of needing two minutes to finish my task. Throughout this chapter, I have told you stories of learners counting eggs, avocados, and shoelaces. Seconds are intangible, abstract units that you can neither see nor touch. Shoelaces, by contrast, you can hold in your hands and manipulate. There is a third type of unit—one that *could* be real but which does not yet exist. This is a story about that third kind of unit.

One of my happiest places to be is at Math On-A-Stick, a large-scale family math

FIGURE 4.17
A Pattern Machine

event at the Minnesota State Fair that I helped to found along with the Minnesota State Fair Foundation and the Minnesota Council of Teachers of Mathematics. For twelve days at the end of each summer, we offer over a dozen different playful math opportunities for children of all ages (adults are invited to play as well!). One of our activities is a table full of Pattern Machines.

A Pattern Machine (see Figure 4.17) starts out as a commercially available set of mechanical flash cards. Nine rows of nine buttons pop up and down like the ends of clicky ballpoint pens. In the original version, each button has two factors on top and their product on the front. You are supposed to push one button at a time to practice your multiplication facts, as you would use flash cards. See "6 x 3," think "18," and then pop up the button to check your work. We covered up the buttons with colorful sign vinyl to encourage children to play with patterning, counting, and other creative pursuits.

One morning at Math On-A-Stick, a five-year-old girl had the Pattern Machine table to herself: one girl and about twenty machines. Her mother was relaxing nearby, but the girl was all business making things on the Pattern Machines.

On closer observation, I noticed that she made something on one machine, then left it and moved to another. Over the course of fifteen or twenty minutes, she moved from one end of the eight-foot table to the other, leaving behind a trail of Pattern Machines— each in a different state (Figure 4.18).

I talked with her mother and learned that they had just come from the stunt dog show

FIGURE 4.18
A trail of Pattern Machines

at the fair, which the daughter had found positively delightful. The girl was now using the Pattern Machines to imagine pens for the stunt dogs to run around in between shows. She had begun with two pens, vertically divided (leftmost in Figure 4.19), moved on to more than two pens, then to horizontal divisions (center), and finally began working on dividing the pens both horizontally and vertically (rightmost in Figure 4.19).

While I have no evidence that this five-year-old was *counting* the number

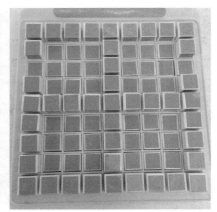

FIGURE 4.19
Pens for stunt dogs

 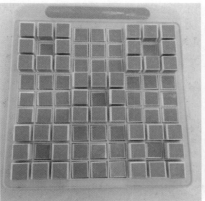 

FIGURE 4.20
Would each of these make a good pen for stunt dogs?

of different ways she could make pens for these dogs, she was definitely imagining them. There is a branch of mathematics—*combinatorics*—that concerns itself with counting the number of ways various events can happen or that various objects can be combined. If you have ever wondered how many different ways there are for you to get from home to work or how many different combinations a combination lock can have, then you've thought about combinatorics. This girl had posed and was working to solve an original and well-defined combinatorics problem—What are all the ways these machines can be subdivided to make pens for stunt dogs?

Despite (or because of?) the girl's deep engagement in this problem, I couldn't resist the temptation to get a slightly deeper view of her thinking. So I asked about what counts as a pen. Starting with the leftmost machine in Figure 4.20, I asked whether each would make good pens for the dogs. She agreed that the one on the left would work just fine. The one in the middle she pronounced adequate as a "sitting pen," and the one on the right elicited an eyeroll and a sigh. Whether she was literally counting these possibilities or not, she had done the important counting work of precisely defining (in her own mind) the unit to be counted—configurations of pens containing at least one button, without gaps in the borders—and she was working to bring these different possibilities into being. She was keeping track of something between intangible abstract units, such as seconds, and concrete units, such as shoelaces—she was keeping track of *possibilities*.

THE EFFECTS OF *HOW MANY?* IN YOUR CLASSROOM

This chapter has been about learning through counting. The images in *How Many?* are a starting place—a set of examples for viewing the intellectual world of counting in a richer way that reveals new possibilities.

After a number of *How Many?* conversations, you and your students should begin to see new relationships in the world. New answers to old textbook tasks. New units in your classroom. New ways of grouping the objects you encounter or imagine as you work and play. You may find yourselves less concerned with right answers to questions involving "how many?" and more focused on finding creative and surprising answers. At least, this has been my experience at home, in schools, and elsewhere. I hope it will be yours.

CHAPTER 5
Answers Key

I was reluctant to provide an answer key for *How Many?* because every image has many right answers, and I worried that neglecting to mention a particular response in an answer key could signal that I thought it was wrong. Conversely, any answer I do provide could seem to be of greater value to the reader than answers not given here. Yet, I do want to equip teachers for the wide range of possible responses that each image may provoke. It is in this spirit that I offer an answers key (with plural *answers*). For each page in the student book, here are some common—and some not-so-common—responses to the question, *How Many?*

Possible answers on each page are listed in numerical order.

$\frac{1}{2}$ of an apple

1 half-apple

1 star

1 tiny circle at the center
of the apple

1 circular green ring at
the apple's edge

2 circles—1 big, 1 tiny

4 colors (green, brown,
white, and red)

5 seeds

5 seed compartments

10 light green dots
surrounding the seeds

40 letters on the cover

How Many?

A COUNTING BOOK / CHRISTOPHER DANIELSON

$\frac{1}{8}$ of the apple per slice
  (not counting the core)

1 stem

1 core

1 apple slicer

1 apple

1 circular blade for
  cutting out the apple's
  core

1 tabletop

2 handles

6 strips of wood on the
  table's surface

8 straight blades for
  cutting the apple

8 apple slices

1 pair of shoes

1 box

1 12-sided polygon (a dodecagon, shaped like a plus sign)

2 holes in the box's top

2 semicircles cut from the ends of the box

2 shoelaces

2 shoes

2 flaps on the box top

2 different lacing schemes (the left-footed shoe has the ends of the shoelaces going from top to bottom of the top set of eyelets; the right-footed shoe has them going from bottom to top)

3 lines of text on the box top

4 aglets

12 sides on the dodecagon

20 eyelets

About 40 yellow stitches on each shoe (of which about 20 are visible on each shoe)

About 50 small holes visible in the insoles of the two shoes combined

Ever since 1 April 1960, when Dr. Martens boots first rolled off the production line and onto the feet of postmen, policemen and everyday workers, our reputation for durability has become footwear folklore. Over 100 million pairs later, our belief in making things to last is as strong as it's ever been.

0 shoes

0 shoelaces

0 eyelets

0 aglets

0 elephants (although to be fair, nearly every page of this book has 0 elephants)

1 box

2 footprints

2 bold black bars in the footprints

$\frac{1}{12}$ of a dozen eggs

$\frac{11}{12}$ of a dozen eggs missing

1 egg carton

1 egg

1 dozen egg cups

2 knobs on the flap on the front of the egg carton

2 holes for the knobs to protrude through

2 rows of 6 egg cups

4 holes in the top of the egg carton

5 posts separating the eggs

6 pairs of egg cups

11 empty egg cups

12 egg cups altogether

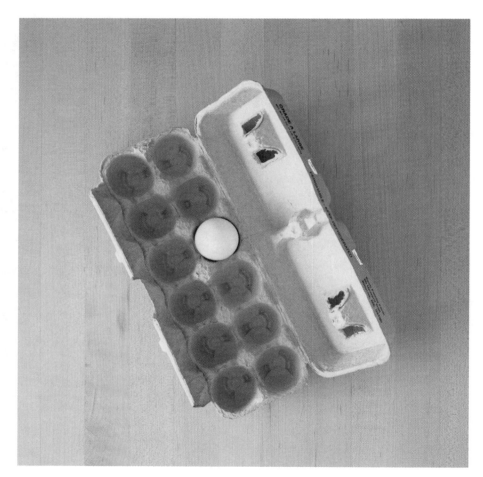

1 dozen eggs

1 3-by-4 array

2 groups of 6 eggs

2 eggs in the interior of the carton

3 rows

4 columns

4 corner eggs

6 posts separating the eggs

10 eggs on the boundary of the carton

$\frac{1}{3}$ of a dozen eggs in the frying pan

$\frac{2}{3}$ of a dozen eggs in the carton

1 double-yolked egg

1 frying pan

1 stove burner

1 bowl containing salt

1 bowl containing pepper

2 bowls of condiments

2 burners that the pan appears to span

3 single-yolked eggs

4 fried eggs

4 empty egg cups

4 angled irons visible beneath the pan

5 visible yolks

8 eggshells (or is it 4?)

8 unfried eggs

90

1 red bowl

5 visible stem ends on the grapefruit

6 visible grapefruit (or is it 7? It's difficult to know whether the bit at 4 o'clock is a grapefruit or a reflection)

7 total grapefruit (or 8, depending on how many visible grapefruit you've decided on)

1 cutting board

1 measuring cup

1 citrus reamer

2 half-grapefruits with 12 sections

2 half-grapefruits with 13 sections

2 half-grapefruits with 14 sections

3 rows

4 columns

5 circular holes in each of the uppermost sections of the citrus reamer

6 grapefruit

6 half-grapefruits with 11 sections

7 half-grapefruits with exposed seeds

8 strips of wood in the cutting board

8 splines on the citrus reamer

11 sections in most of the half-grapefruits

12 half-grapefruits

12 sections in the half-grapefruit in the upper left

13 sections in the half-grapefruit in the lower right

14 sections in the half-grapefruit in the upper right

About 15 visible partial or whole seeds

144 grapefruit sections (or maybe half-sections. If you cut a section, do you have 2 sections?)

2 grapefruit rinds

$3\frac{1}{2}$ cups of juice

4 juice glasses

7 grapefruits in the background

7 ounces of juice per glass if shared equally

8 seeds

28 fluid ounces of grapefruit juice

1 uncut avocado
1 cut avocado
1 avocado pit
1 knife
2 avocado halves
2 whole avocados
$\frac{4}{2}$ avocados
3 circles on the handle of
   the knife

1 cutting board
1 mortar
1 pestle
1 lime
1 whole jalapeño
1 tomato
1 onion
1 bunch of cilantro
1 missing avocado half
1 missing pit
2 lime halves
3 rows of avocado halves
5 jalapeño slices
5 leaflets on the tomato stem
5 columns of avocado halves
7 pits
7 downward-pointing avocado halves
$\frac{15}{2}$ avocados
$7\frac{1}{2}$ avocados
8 divots
8 upward-pointing avocado halves
15 half-avocados

1 pizza wheel

2 rows of pizzas

3 toppings (or 4 if you count cheese)

3 columns of pizzas

4 green pepper slices

4 lobes on each green pepper slice

4 visible sauce spots on the upper left pizza

4 types of pizza

6 pizzas

9 mushroom slices

11 pepperoni slices on the pizza in the top row

12 pepperoni slices on the pizza in the bottom row

31 circles (the 6 pizzas, the 23 pepperoni slices, the pizza wheel, and the center of the pizza wheel)

$\frac{1}{6}$ of a pizza per slice

$\frac{1}{3}$ of a pizza per serving

1 plate

2 cut pizzas

2 slices of pizza per serving

3 cuts per pizza (if the cuts go from edge to edge of the pizza)

4 uncut pizzas

5 slices remaining in each cut pizza

6 cuts per pizza (if the cuts go from the center to the edge of the pizza)

6 total cuts (if the cuts go from edge to edge; 12 if they go from center to edge)

6 slices per pizza

12 slices

18 two-slice servings

60 degrees (approximately) in the angle of each slice of pizza

$\frac{1}{2}$ dozen eggs

$\frac{1}{2}$ avocado

$\frac{1}{2}$ glass of grapefruit juice

$\frac{1}{2}$ of a pizza

$\frac{1}{2}$ of a pair of shoes

1 dozen half-eggs

1 towel

1 bowl

1 pitcher

1 dishwasher

1 visible shelf

2 quarter-pizzas

2 drawer pulls

2 visible knobs on the cabinets

4 layers in the folded towel

10 visible holes in the shelf support

13 holes in the shelf support, including the ones hidden by the shelf

1 pair of dozens of eggs
1 pair of halved avocados
1 pair of grapefruit
1 pair of pizza slices
1 pair of shoes
1 pair of half-pears
1 pear
1 halved pear seed
2 colors of eggs
2 avocado pits
2 egg cartons
4 avocado shells
4 pieces of green pepper
4 holes in the egg
  cartons
12 brown eggs
12 white eggs
24 eggs

$\frac{7}{8}$ of an apple pie
1 pie plate
1 missing slice of pie
About 1 dozen crumbs
5 vents in the pie's crust
7 remaining slices of
   apple pie

1 small plate

1 small fork

1 large plate

1 large fork

1 book

2 blue plates

2 forks

3 missing slices of pie

3 visible vents in the pie's crust

4 tines on each fork

5 remaining slices of pie

8 total fork tines

∞ images of the book's back cover

BONUS CHALLENGE

If you wish, you can read this book like a traditional counting book by finding one thing in the first image, two things in the second image, and so on. This is a challenging task that will require perseverance and creativity. Here is one way to complete the challenge:

1 pair of shoes

2 footprints

3 sets of four egg cups in the carton

4 columns of three eggs each

5 yolks

6 clearly visible grapefruit

7 half-grapefruits with exposed seeds

8 grapefruit seeds on the counter

9 horizontal edges on the dark boards making up the cutting board

10 green things beneath the cutting board (5 jalapeño slices, 1 whole jalapeño, 2 half-limes, a bunch of cilantro, and the tomato's stem)

11 pepperoni slices on the top center pizza

12 slices total in the 2 cut pizzas

13 holes for mounting the shelf beneath the counter in the foreground (you can see 10 of them, and careful measurement reveals that there is space behind the shelf for 3 more)

14 things on the counter top: 2 grapefruit, 2 dozen eggs, 4 half-avocado shells, 2 avocado pits, 2 slices of pizza, and 2 pear halves

References

Carpenter, Thomas P., Elizabeth Fennema, Megan Loef Franke, Linda Levi, and Susan B. Empson. 2014. *Children's Mathematics: Cognitively Guided Instruction.* 2nd ed. Portsmouth, NH: Heinemann.

Carpenter, Thomas P., Megan Loef Franke, Nicholas C. Johnson, Angela C. Turrou, and Anita A. Wager. 2016. *Young Children's Mathematics: Cognitively Guided Instruction in Early Childhood Education.* Portsmouth, NH: Heinemann.

Davis, Rafranz. 2014. "Math Talks with Braeden: Investigations Matter." March 19. www.rafranzdavis.com/math-talks-with-braeden-investigations-matter/

Dehaene, Stanislas. 2011. *The Number Sense: How the Mind Creates Mathematics.* Revised ed. Oxford, UK: Oxford University Press.

Fuson, Karen C., Diana Wearne, James C. Hiebert, Hanlie G. Murray, Pieter G. Human, Alwyn I. Olivier, Thomas P. Carpenter, and Elizabeth Fennema. 1997. "Children's Conceptual Structures for Multidigit Numbers and Methods of Multidigit Addition and Subtraction." *Journal for Research in Mathematics Education* 28 (2): 130–162.

Halberda, Justin, Michèle M. M. Mazzocco, and Lisa Feigenson. 2008. "Individual Differences in Non-verbal Number Acuity Correlate with Maths Achievement." *Nature* 455:665–668.

Hoban, Russell. 1964. *Bread and Jam for Frances.* New York: Harper and Row.

Humphreys, Cathy, and Ruth Parker. 2015. *Making Number Talks Matter: Developing Mathematical Practices and Deepening Understanding, Grades 4–10.* Portland, ME: Stenhouse.

Park, Joonkoo, and Elizabeth M. Brannon. 2013. "Training the Approximate Number System Improves Math Proficiency." *Psychological Science* 24 (10): 2013–3019.

Parrish, Sherry. 2010. *Number Talks: Helping Children Build Mental Math and Computation Strategies.* Sausalito, CA: Math Solutions.

Philipp, Randolph. 2008. "Motivating Prospective Elementary Teachers to Learn Mathematics by Focusing on Children's Mathematical Thinking" (unpublished manuscript).

Philipp, Randolph, Candace Cabral, and Bonnie P. Schappelle. 2005. *IMAP: Integrating Mathematics and Pedagogy to Illustrate Children's Mathematical Thinking.* Upper Saddle River, NJ: Pearson.